I0088306

An Unusual Childhood

An Unusual Childhood
Growing up around Jardine, Montana 1916 - 1930
By Harlene Jessie (Reeves) Ritchie
3rd Edition - 2012

With contributions from her children
Designed by Bill H. Ritchie

Ritchie's Perfect Press
A Division of Emeralda Works
500 Aloha #105
Seattle WA 98109
(206) 498-9208

E-mail ritchie@emeralda.com
Homepage http://www.emeralda.com

No part of this book may be reproduced without expressed
permission of Bill Ritchie.

ISBN 10 1562359053
ISBN 13 9781562359058

Copyright 2012 Bill Ritchie

An Unusual Child-hood

By
Harlene Jessie (Reeves) Ritchie

As written in her own words

Ritchie's Perfect Press - Seattle WA USA

"I believe I had an unusual childhood and in this rushed and harried day of civilization, I wish my own daughters and sons could have had a part of our life, on Eagle Creek, in Montana."

- HJR
Selah, Washington 1993

The two little sisters, about 3 and 2 years old. Sylvia Reeves, left, is 13 months older than Harlene. The picture must have been taken about 1917 or 1918.

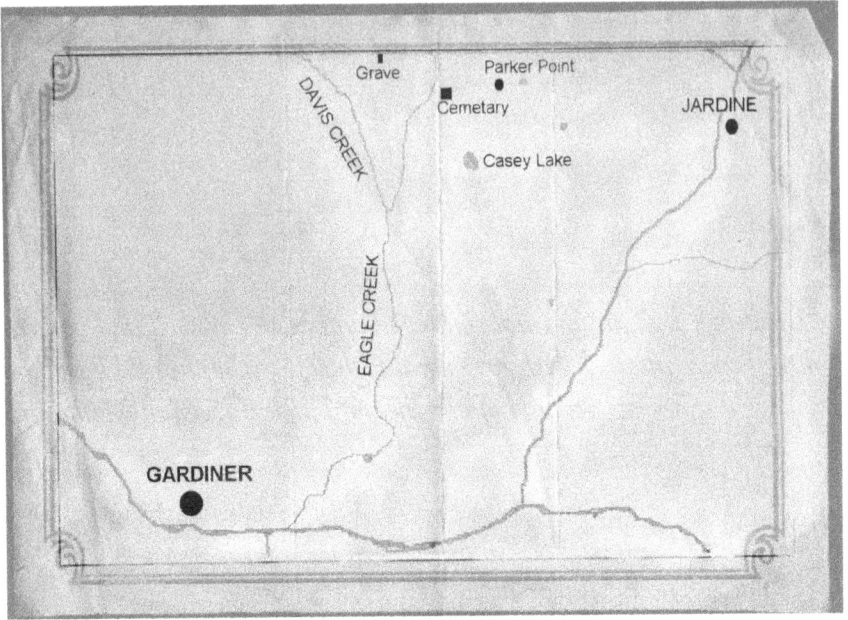

Map of the mountain area where Harlene was born and grew up. Jardine was the nearest settlement. Gardiner was down stream. Her mother's family home - the Davis house - was on Eagle Creek. At the end of her story you may read about her return to the old home sites and what she found there.

Jan 29, 1916

I was born poor, didn't have any attendants at my birth, except my mother and 13-month old sister, Sylvia. Mighty cold in Montana during the winter; my Dad walked out on snowshoes, but didn't get back in time with the doc.

Poor Daddy — another girl. So I got my name, Harlene Jessie. I was ordered from the Sears Roebuck Catalog, as all my brothers and Sylvia were.

We lived on the homestead, Buffalo Flats - way out yonder, no neighbors and lots of rattlers. So we had lots of pigs (they kill snakes), and Mom had typhoid fever.

She hated the crowded log cabin and the loneliness, so we moved to Grandpa Davis' house, on Eagle Creek. I don't know where Grandpa and Grandma went; probably Grandpa couldn't stand the kids. No telling where poor grandma had to live; she was

Burley in the wgon, Harlene in teh foreground and Sylvia behind.

accustomed to moving on. Anyway we had the 160 acres and range rights and the brand "Z6," and cows and horses.

My father worked for other people and at home, though we lived at Cedar Creek for a while, Clyde was born there. He was a great disappointment to Burley and I, as Mom had promised us a surprise and we were sure it would be the Easter Bunny.

Sylvia accepted him as she loved babies, but it was quite some time before Burley and I forgave him. It was here that Sylvia practiced up on life-saving. I fell in a big ditch, she managed to get me by the hair and kept my head from going under and screamed till Mom came to the rescue.

This is sort of a mixed up story, as I can't remember some of the places we stayed, I know that when Burley was yet a baby, our father got the job of babysitting a car load of cattle to the Chicago stockyards, and since it wasn't too far from his old home at Wycliffe, Kentucky, Mom and her brood, Sylvia, Burley and I traveled by train to accompany our father.

It was there that we had a bag of oranges to eat on the train, and it burst open, rolling oranges everywhere on the depot platform, with Sylvia and I scrambling after them, under peoples' feet and it was some time before we and the oranges were rounded up. Mom and we young ones were put on the train to Kentucky and our father parted with us to complete the task of getting the cattle delivered, and then he vanished.

This was the year of the great flu epidemic that killed thousands, sometimes, whole families. Our father had been feeling bad, and managed to deliver the cattle, then passed out, a stranger in a strange town.

Someone got him into a hotel room, and finding his train fare to Kentucky on him, got him aboard. So he arrived home, deathly ill and with a frightened wife and three youngsters, his Mom was none too glad to see us, she had a house full of sick people, and being a widow, was not prepared for guests.

Harlene Jessie Reeves

My Mom didn't like her strange mother-in-law, who spoke with the accent of the Deep South, and the feeling was mutual, but they had to make the best of it as Daddy had gone into a coma and everyone was sure he wouldn't live.

This was a bad time, although I didn't realize it, I liked the attention I got. Sylvia made herself obnoxious to her aunts and uncle Clyde by crying and screaming, I guess she wanted to go home. We had to stay there until Daddy recovered enough to travel, it must have been quite a long time, as he was weaker than one of his children.

Harley Reeves as a young man.

This was the last time Daddy saw his mother.

We returned to Gardiner, Montana and back to the Eagle Creek ranch. It was here that our parents often left us at the house, while they worked together, clearing brush and young trees, so more hay could be grown. Often we saw bears, and once the ranger came by on horseback and told Mom to keep us indoors as a bull buffalo was in our field. We watched him grazing for what seemed hours, until he wandered away.

We were always cautioned to stay indoors while our parents worked, but it was tiresome, so one day Sylvia and I made our way through the timber and up a hill, where we could hear the axes at work and Daddy's voice as he urged the horses to drag trees off the cleared land. They were quite surprised to see Sylvia and me. We were soundly scolded as the danger of bears was real; we were very near Yellowstone Park.

9

An Unusual Childhood

"It's all right," I told my father, "Sylv's got a stick." She was still practicing her life saving techniques.

One day we were taken with our parents, Mom had made fresh bread, so we had our lunch of fresh bread and bacon sandwiches. It was a sunny day and Sylv (Sylvia), Burl (Burley), Clyde and I spent the day peeling the bark off freshly cut trees, poking at the fire that Mom had made, burning the branches.

I went to sleep in the sun, and was wakened by Mom. She was ready to go to the house, it was near evening, so she had to carry Clyde home, and Sylv and Burl had gone down the trail long before. It was nearly dark when we reached the house and Mom started supper immediately, she said something about Sylv and Burl had probably gone on to the barn to wait for Daddy and the horses. Clyde went to sleep in a chair; Mom was putting the food on when Daddy and Sylv came in to get the milk pail.

"Where's Burl?" Daddy asked. Mom was surprised.

"I thought he was at the barn," so Sylv said. Burl didn't come home with her, he wanted to stop and wade in the creek, so we went on without him. By this time it was dark. Daddy and Mom both set out to find Burl, leaving Sylv in charge. We were supposed to go to bed after we had our supper, but we didn't. Clyde slept, partly on the table and partly on his chair. We were scared, Sylv and I. We were afraid a bear had taken Burl.

Burl and I were good friends most of the time, except when he claimed a brown corduroy dress as being his and it really was mine. I had really outgrown it and Mom let Burl wear it.

He still thinks it was his.

Mom and Daddy came back and Daddy told Mom to stay; he saddled his horse and galloped over the bridge in the dark, going to our nearest neighbors a mile away. Their name was Parker, Jim and old Jim, the grandpa. Mom told us our dog was gone, too, so Burl probably had stayed with the dog.

Harlene Jessie Reeves

The Parkers had a big house and a guest house. They ran a non-efficient dude ranch, as they didn't think much of work such as our Dad did. The mother, Olive, was a sweet humble person, pregnant most of the time, with girls and one fragile boy. The girls' language was a mixture of nice manners and mule skinners' oaths. They were beautiful girls, we were always glad to have them come to play with us.

We especially liked Perry, the sick little boy, he was such a good little boy, and avoided fighting as he never felt good enough to quarrel. The father kept a lady friend in their guest house, and when Mrs. P. came to visit Mom she would cry about he lady guest. Mom sympathized with her; we wondered why. It seemed a good idea for someone to live so near that they could visit back and forth without saddling a horse or hitching up a team.

I don't know who found Burley, but he had crossed the creek and followed the dog, and was all right. It was a long night, though. I still remember the homemade bread we ate, Clyde sleeping on his chair.

The house we lived in at that time was of logs, with an up-stairs, where there were two bedrooms. One of the rooms, we were afraid of; we called it the blue room, as it had blue wallpaper. Daddy had caught a half-grown coyote, he hoped to tame it, so had locked it in the blue room, where it raged and tore at the walls, until Daddy gave up the project and got rid of the coyote, but we were still afraid of the blue room. We would go up the stairs and rush into the other room, slamming the door, outwitting whatever we were afraid of in the blue room.

We had a huge black piano; it had big legs and claw feet, with glass knobs under the claws. It was a good hiding place. Once when our parents were out, three men, clad in cowboy clothes came. They knocked on the door, so all four we brave youngsters squeezed behind the piano, I had the outside place, so I could see the riders come in the house. They were talking of waiting for our folks. One of them came over to the piano and started trying to play it. His back was closed to me, and to my horror I recognized his chaps.

11

An Unusual Childhood

He was Horace LaBree, an Indian who worked part time for Jim Parker. We all held our breath, scared silly. The men finally left, and later on I found out that they knew we were behind the piano all the time.

We were really afraid of H. LaBree; he was sort of a mean person, although Geraldine Parker didn't think so. Once, when we were visiting Parkers, we found a batch of kittens in their barn. H. LaBree got a gunny sack, put the kittens in it, got an ax, laid the sack on a stump and pounded the sacked kittens all to pieces. Geraldine laughed, but we had nightmares about dead cats afterwards.

WINFRED H. DAVIS, LICENSED GUIDE, JARDINE, MONT.
Elk, Deer, Mountain Sheep, Bear.

This photo turned up in Sylvia's collection of memorabilia, showing a picture of Harley's father-in-law, Winfred Davis and a party of Dudes.

Geraldine was a real tomboy, she did anything she wanted to, and paid no attention to her gentle mother. We liked Ruth Ellen and Amy, but there were times when they were quite mean, too.

Another time when our parents had gone to Gardiner for a supply of groceries, we got Mom's wedding dress out of the closet and took turns wearing it, holding it up in front and dragging it about in the dirt in the yard. Mom was really unhappy about it, so we each had a going over with Daddy's razor strop.

I'll never forget that leather strop. It taught us to obey orders, and to think before acting. We all had another taste of it when we cut Daddy's life insurance policy into little squares, pretending they were film and tried to take pictures with them.

One day in August, Burl, Clyde and I were in the chicken house, roosting on the roosts and cackling whenever one of us produced an imaginary egg, Sylv came running in to tell us a new baby was at the house. Mrs. Parker was there and Mom chose this uncooperative time to be sick in bed, so Mrs. Parker had to cook the meals and take care of the new baby, Bud, and even wait on Mom, making tea for her and was so nice, she even darned the holes in our stockings.

Sears Roebuck was very nice to us; besides sending us the baby, they sent a lot of baby clothes, too. Bud was a lot of fun. We all took care of him, although he liked Sylv the best. He called her "Toe." The rest of us had to wash his clothes, as Mom told us the dirty diapers would make our hands soft and white.

My father went to work in the gold mine at Jardine, and came home on the weekends. He brought candy and groceries, dried apples and apricots and canned milk, although we did have a milk cow. During the week, Mom did all the chores, and we had to learn to milk the cow and help feed the work horses.

Another job we had was to take a can of poisoned oats, and a big spoon and wander all over the fields, putting a spoonful of oats in every gopher hole. The gophers not only destroyed the crops, but made holes, dangerous for a horse to step into.

When spring came, Daddy came home to the ranch. He had a lot to do, fixing the fences, turning water on the big field and he and Mom would go out on the range, past Grey Donkey, a mountain ridge, where there were wild horses roaming loose and without owners. One at a time they would rope one and lead it rearing and fighting, back to the ranch, where they were turned loose in the big corral. This was tiring work, as each horse was different, and they had to be broken to ride.

My folks didn't believe in letting the horse buck until its spirit was broken, they would tie their legs until the horse lay down helplessly, then would put the saddle blanket on, after letting the frightened horse smell and see it. After that he would be allowed to sniff the saddle, and it was put on. Then the feet were untied and the horse was closely tied to old Pat, or another stable saddle horse, his head was tied high so he couldn't buck, then another quiet saddle horse was tied to the wild one, so he was led between 2 saddle horses.

Usually there was a struggle to get loose and throw the saddle off, but finally he would calm down and walk quietly between the two gentle ones. Later a rider would get on the wild one, when one of the tame ones went without a rider. A few days of this treatment, we had a green broken horse, either Mom or Daddy would ride them a lot, keeping a tight reign and watching for action. Eventually, we would have another gentle horse.

We had two, though, who gave their lives. One was Peggy, a blue roan, a beautiful thing, but stubborn, she refused to lead or anything. My father tied her to a post in the corral. During the night she went round and round that post fighting it, in the morning she was dead, with a broken neck.

We had a beautiful red roan, a good runner, tall and slim. He got out and re-joined the wild ones. My parents looked for Ted; he was worth a lot and partly broken. They never found him, but saw one like him and fought him all the way home.

He was turned into the corral, where he ran and reared banging against the poles. Finally he threw himself at the fence, sharp ends of a pole, running it into his belly he bled to death, biting and fighting to the end. He was dragged away to join Peggy, in a gulch, where the coyotes took over. That was the last time we named a horse Ted.

14

Harlene Jessie Reeves

Once when Mom was out riding, checking horses, she found a dead mare, with a tiny colt still standing beside her. Mom put the little thing across her horse and brought it home. It was too weak to drink, so Mom tried to feed it with a bottle. It became weaker, until it couldn't stand, so Mom rigged up a sling so its feet could touch the floor, and kept trying to save it, but it was no use. The poor little thing joined the other dead.

Sylvia, Naomi (Davis) Reeves, little Burley and Harlene at the Cedar Creek place.

Another unlucky animal, Black Bear, a black steer, died suddenly. According to the vet book it had black leg. The book advised burning, or burying, to keep this contagious disease from spreading. It would have taken a mighty bit hole to bury the steer, so Daddy dragged it away piled branches and wood on it and started it burning. It took several days, and whenever the wind blew from that direction, it was almost more than we could stand.

We had a playhouse, one that grandpa Winfred Davis had made for Mom and her sisters. It was made of logs, like a miniature log cabin, we didn't like to play in it much, as there was some old doll clothes left in it and they were rotting and part of the dirt floor, we imagined some poor child had died there and the clothes were all

15

that was left. Sylv had a wild imagination; she told us stories, which we believed.

From our home, we could see a distant mountain peak, Crevasse, by name. She told us that people went there and jumped, or fell to their deaths. I always thought of a line of people climbing that mountain, so they could jump off. Often at night, when the coyotes howled, I could see these poor people jumping from that peak.

Another tale my sister told us was to listen to the "lost sound", the wind in the tall spruce trees. I still like to listen to the "lost sound."

Spring came to the ranch, with the gold of sun flowers, everywhere, and every kind of wild flower: Johnny Jump-ups, Wild Violets, Buttercups, Clover blooms, Wild Geraniums, Flags, Cowslips, Forget-me-nots, many others we didn't know the names of and, in the deep dark part of the woods, the perfect Avalanche Lily and Wild Orchids.

Then there were edible Dutchman Britches and Wild Rhubarb. Many other edible plants grew, some were bulbs that we pulled up and ate raw, and others were to be cooked as spinach. Even the wild thistle was cut off, peeled, sliced in salt and vinegar, and very good.

Spring was a wonderful time; we wove flower head bands and charms and forgot to come in to lunch. There also was the wild roses and another white flowering shrub, later it produced berries. We had wild gooseberries, for pies, with lots of sugar. Later, when they ripened, Sylv mixed the juice, and lots of sugar and water, which she hid in the roots of a fallen tree. It made a good substitute for Kool-Aid—unknown at that time.

Mom planted a garden; we earned a nickel a row to weed it. Then we filled up on raw peas, little new carrots and strawberries. Mom had to take care of things at home, the cow and a few horses, most of them were out on range lands, and the cows were in a pasture near the house

Harlene Jessie Reeves

Mrs. Parker came to see us and brought Perry. He and four of us played in the creek, finding bright new rocks, but Perry got a nose bleed and they had to go home.

One day that summer, Mr. Parker rode in and told us that Perry was dead. She was very unhappy, as Perry was the only boy. He was buried not far from this house, with four little evergreen trees planted around the little grave.

We didn't see the Parker girls for some time after Perry's death. Mrs. Parker and the girls moved to another one of their houses, they usually had city people in. We were closer then, so sometimes Mom would let us go to play with the girls.

We were always given scissors and a catalog to cut out pictures. One day Amy got mad and threw the scissors down the toilet hole (all toilets were outdoor types). We tried to hook the scissors but couldn't, so Ruth-Ellen volunteered to squeeze down the hole if we would hold her feet so she couldn't fall, and to pull her back up when she got the scissors.

Mrs. Parker came just in time to rescue her daughter from a terrible fate. The scissors were off-limits, and Mrs. Parker gave us a different pair. Amy was scolded, but she scolded right back.

During the summer, when the haying, plowing and such, were done, we went away into the mountains, pack horses loaded with camping gear, to Bear Creek, where Daddy was digging a ditch to run water to our ranch, which got pretty dry during the summer.

This ditch came from Bear Creek, through a stand of heavy tall timber, across some of Parker's land and across Teddy's hill. It needed a lot of work; we would all work at shoveling and chopping out the roots. We found some good clay and made figures and marbles, which we baked in the camp fire.

After lunch, Daddy set up a tent and arranged his camp gear, and bedding. He climbed a tree and nailed a pole across to another tree, and with a system of ropes and a pulley, swing his box of groceries in the middle of the cross pole. That way, the bears couldn't get the food, even if they did climb the trees. Mom gathered us and we set out for home.

We had a nice gentle fat mare, Lady, there was room for two of us on her nice soft back, but we hated to ride her because she was so wide our legs stuck way out and by the time we got home we could hardly walk for a while.

We left Daddy there to work alone on the ditch, all hard work, done by hand. I was afraid of this trail; it ran through thick, tall timber, always cool and dark, even in the middle of the day.

There was a bird that seemed to keep just ahead in the trees; it would call "Phoebe?" Also on our way, we passed a tiny log cabin where an old prospector lived alone. We called him "The Austrian," as he was hoping to strike it rich, so he could send for his family in Austria. We never knew his real name.

There was a cold spring in the cow pasture, it came up out of the earth, with moss around it, and was so good and cold it made our teeth hurt. Daddy had made a ditch for it, so it formed a tiny stream that went below the barn and into Eagle Creek. We got our house water from Eagle Creek.

It was cold too, and the creek chattered over its rocks, a pleasant sound that we loved. Our milk, butter and other perishables were kept in a shallow box that was partly filled with water running from the creek. It was covered with netting to keep insects out. Everything from this refrigeration system was icy cold, like big pans of milk, with cream on top; and home made butter, pressed into a square by pressing it in a butter mold when it was freshly churned. The mold had a clover design, so when the butter was removed, it had the clover imprint on it.

Another thing kept in the cold running water was a watermelon, which we enjoyed once per summer, as they were imported from another state and very expensive. Our father told us about the melons growing in Kentucky when he was a boy, and we envied the people who had all the melons they could eat.

18

Harlene Jessie Reeves

One summer we had an unusually big green-striped melon. Daddy told Burley to bring it up from the creek. On his way back with the cold dripping melon, poor Burl couldn't hold it and dropped it in the dirt. It was a real ripe one, so it split into several pieces. We were sure Burl would get the razor strap, but he didn't. Mom salvaged all she could, and made watermelon pickles out of the rind.

We also had cottage cheese from the extra milk we couldn't use, and there were times the cows got into a patch of wild garlic, no one could drink this garlic flavored milk, so we went without for a while. I don't know why we didn't drink Sylv's gooseberry wine.

Finally, Sylv and I were old enough to start school, at least Sylv was six and I wanted to do whatever she did. As we were too far from a school, and were snowbound during the winter, we went to Mrs. Parker's. She had some training as a teacher and was teaching her own children. Mom would put us on a horse, and taking Burl with her on her horse, we rode to Parker's. Our father usually stayed with Bud and Clyde until she got back.

After our school day was over, we were put on our horse, and he came home by himself. We became quite independent, going back and forth by ourselves. After we had learned the way, we could walk to and from the Parker's. Even after some snow had fallen we bundled up and went to school. We liked it there at Parker's; they had a lot of expensive toys, including a dandy rocking horse.

Mrs. Parker always made us take off our long black stockings and hung them up to dry, as we usually managed to get our feet wet. She always had cookies for us. She was one of the kindest people I have ever known.

One evening after a snow fall, we were going home when we saw huge man-like foot prints. They had come from above the road, crossed the road, and down into the brush along a small creek. Sylv and I took off running for home, out of breath and in record time we got home. Daddy got his horse and went to see for himself, and when he returned, reported the tracks were a bear's, and probably a big one at that. This was the end of our first grade.

An Unusual Childhood

Winter came in full force; snow every day and the temperature dropped as low as 30 below zero. Out in the timber, large trees went "bang" in the night, they were split by the rapidly dropping temperatures. Every morning our doors were blocked by new snow, it was cleared away, and eventually the paths to barn and hay stacks were several feet deep. Clyde could walk in them and only the top of his head showed.

It was a lot of work feeding the cows and horses. Daddy had built a high fence around the hay stacks to keep the stray elk from jumping over to get the hay. Also the ice had to be broken in the creek, so all the animals could drink. Then the water would overflow and freeze another layer of ice so there was layer after layer of ice stacked up. Huge icicles formed at the eaves of the house, they were solid and big as a person at their top and reached to the snow at the bottom, forming a greenish tunnel between the house wall, and the ice walls.

One day when it turned sunny, Mom let Sylv and I go out. We went along the house wall in the nice green ice tunnel, when there was a grinding roar, and a whole section of roof snow softened and ice, snow and all came down on our heads. Mom thought we were killed, but we were only stunned and recovered quickly.

Mom spent lots of the winter re-sewing clothes for all of us. We wore hand-made moccasins made from deer skin with furry tops. Daddy put out a trap line, and caught several types of fur-bearing animals. They were carefully skinned; the skins turned inside-out and stretched on boards to dry.

The coyote skins sold at a cheap price, but weasel skins were expensive, as they turned snow white in the winter, with a black tip on their tails. They sold as Ermine, and smelled terrible while being skinned. We never pitied the ermine or weasel, as they were sneaky, blood thirsty animals. They would even get in the chicken house and the stupid chickens would just sit there and let the weasel bite into their veins and suck their blood away. When the chicken woke up it was too late, they would tumble off their roosts—dead. One weasel could kill several chickens in one night.

Harlene Jessie Reeves

I had no pity for either the chickens or the weasels. I was afraid of feathers anyway. We visited a lady at Gardiner, she had a baby too young to walk. This mother put honey on the baby's hands and then gave him some feathers to play with. He sat there and pulled the sticky mess from one hand to the other, and was amused for a long time. We tried it on Bud, only used molasses instead of honey.

He picked at the feathers for awhile, then got mad and started screaming. Mom was angry with us, she cleaned the sticky mess off Bud's hands and he was happy again.

The winters were long and tiresome. Some days we couldn't go outdoors, and the big pot-bellied stove glowed with heat. Daddy would bring in a big load of wood, pile it way high in the wood box, and both the kitchen range and the heater were kept going. Frost formed on the window glass, making beautiful pictures of ferns and flowers. We knew that Jack Frost had come in the night and arranged the pictures.

It was so cold we had to keep turning our backs to heater, then fronts to heater. The area away from the heater and cooking range was icy. Even the water pail had a layer of ice on top. It seemed as if we were extra hungry, eating stew of vegetables from the cellar and elk meat, or chicken, and stewed dried apples or apricots--sometimes made into pies. Mom would bring out a huge fruit cake, dark and moist.

We had honey in five gallon cans, it got so cold and thick it would hardly pour, but we could eat pieces off it for our sour-dough hot-cakes and home-made bread or biscuits. Daddy would always order sorghum when we got our winter groceries. We would take a bit of butter and sorghum and stir them together for an unusually good spread.

We had our own bacon and ham and eggs, milk and plenty of canned elk meat. Also Mom had apple sauce and apple butter, wild blackberry jam and tiny sweet pickles made from the little pea-shaped radishes. Near Christmas, we would get a lot of hard candy and new stockings, from good old Sears Roebuck.

21

An Unusual Childhood

Either Mom or Daddy would ride to Jardine to get our package. If the snow was too deep, or crusted for the horse, Daddy would put on snowshoes and walk after the mail. Christmas was a wonderful time. We had trees all over the place and had plenty of choices. Our tree reached the ceiling, fresh and green; we had strings of popcorn on it, and paper chains of red and green. Then there were the twinkling candles all over the tree.

We were cautioned about moving the candles, as they were carefully placed so the little flames couldn't reach the tree needles.

Then there were the toys! Brightly-painted tops, made from Moms spools, and carved wooden animals, also brightly painted. For Sylv and I there were new rag dolls, with shoe button eyes and hair made of pieces of elk skin sewed on top. They had extra clothes and little patch work quilts.

In our socks were peanuts, hard candy and an apple. My parents had let Sylv go to Gardiner, as she had to start school. She lived with Mr. and Mrs. (Ray and Jean) Ritchie. They were very nice to her, and brought her home for Christmas. They had given her a doll. It was beautiful, had jointed arms and legs. Its eyes could open and close and it had real hair.

My doll was of rags, stuffed with cotton, and it had stiff elk-colored hair. I threw it down and screamed and wouldn't shut up till Mom threatened me with the razor strap. Jean Ritchie tried to tell me that my doll was much the prettiest, but I knew better. The Ritchie's went back to Gardiner, leaving Sylvia home during the Christmas vacation.

Just before Jean Ritchie left, she got Sylvia by one of her long braids and told Mom to make her help with the housework. Mom did start having Sylv do more of the work, and she started to pretend she was a grown-up lady. She took care of Bud a lot.

Winter seemed to drag on and on. Mom began to worry that the canned food was getting low—also the oil for our lamps and lanterns—so they decided to go to Gardiner for more supplies. They got the team and sleigh ready and put hot irons in the quilts around their feet to keep from freezing. We couldn't go with them, as it was much too cold. Daddy put plenty of wood in the big heater, shutting the damper so it would burn slowly to keep the house warm while they were gone.

Mom told Sylv that she was in charge of us and to give us our lunch, and what to feed Bud. Then away they went, all bundled up against the cold, with the big work horses plunging through the deep snowdrifts. We played around down stairs, but when Sylv took Bud upstairs to put him to bed, we all went with her.

Bud wouldn't go to sleep, so Sylv said if we took our shoes off we could play in the big bed with Bud. We made tents with the covers and played peek-a-boo with Bud. We dug in the dresser drawers and looked at Mom's diamond. Daddy had bought it for Mom; it was set in a broach. Mom didn't wear it much, but kept it in its little box in a drawer. She was afraid she might lose it if she wore it much.

Clyde and Burl found a box of matches. They had always been trained to not touch matches, they knew matches would burn. Sylv was trying to get Bud to sleep, but he wouldn't stay laid down but kept pushing away the covers and sitting up. I had a pair of scissors and had cut a lot of pictures out of the Sears Roebuck catalog.

Clyde and Burl had the box of matches and were lighting them, letting them burn right up to their fingers before blowing them out. Finally one of the boys let the match burn too close to his fingers, and he jerked away, the match flew against the wall and into a torn piece of wall paper. Sylv saw it burning the paper and yelled at me and Burley to run downstairs and bring up the water pail.

We ran down, into the kitchen and got the pail, only to discover there was only a tiny bit of water left in it. So out the kitchen door we went, slipping and falling on the icy patch to the creek. There was ice on the water hole and we could get only a little water in the pail, the ice was piled high and the water hole too deep for Burl or I to reach.

We made our way back up the icy path. The two of us struggled up the stairs with the pail of water. We forgot to fear the blue

An Unusual Childhood

room and whatever lurked behind the closed door. When we opened the bedroom we saw the whole wall and ceiling were burning and the room was full of smoke. All four of us fled down the stairs, leaving the water pail on the floor. I fell part of the way, cutting my knee.

We four rushed out the front door. On the porch, we stopped, seeing all the deep snow about us. Sylv suddenly remembered Bud in the burning room, turned and fairly flew up the stairs. Bud was sitting on the bed, screaming, "Toe, Toe!" He was too small to walk. Sylv ran into the room and got Bud. He was dressed in a diaper and shirt. Sylv got out of the burning room, but a piece of burning paper fell on her head, and by the time she joined us on the porch, part of her hair had burned off.

At first we didn't know what to do, but when we saw the dirty-brown smoke rising from the house, we turned to our neighbors, a mile away. The snow was as deep as Clyde's head, and all of us were in stocking feet. We tried to run, but the snow was too deep, so we fought our way up the drive, across the big field and to the gate.

The fence between our place and Parkers was here, and I discovered I still had the scissors in my hand. I threw them into a snow drift. Parker's road had been used, so the snow wasn't so bad. We were almost a third of the way to Parker's house, when here came Jim and Granddad Parker, and their team and sleigh. They had seen the smoke rising over the hill, and had started for our place as fast as they could.

Mrs. Parker came running through the snow to meet us; Jim had loaded us aboard and turned to their home. Mrs. Parker was crying and wiping her eyes on her apron. As soon as we were safe in their house, Jim and Granddad Parker turned and sent their horses running back to the burning house. Mrs. Parker made us get out of our snowy, wet clothes, putting some of her own children's dry clothing on us. At about that time, we started crying, not having time to cry sooner.

Sylv was seven years old. When our parents came home, there was only a smoldering mess; the Parkers had stayed to tell them

24

we were safe. What a blow to our folks but I don't think we were worried. We did feel bad because our kittens had burned up. Jim Parker said the crazy kittens had run into the burning house, committing caticide.

Mom felt the loss of the piano most of all, as it had been Grandma Jennie Davis' piano. The neighbors came and brought clothing bedding and cooking utensils. We moved into the small white house where Mrs. Parker and her brood lived in the summer time. It wasn't meant to be used during the winter. Here we were terribly homesick.

One day while Mom was out Sylv and I determined to see what was in two boxes on a high shelf. One was red and white and the other gold and white. We put a chair on another chair and I held them steady while Sylv climbed up and got the boxes. She got down and we opened the boxes.

What a surprise! There were two beautiful China dolls, dressed in tiny perfect clothes, and had long curls. They were jointed at the shoulders, elbows and wrists, also at hips and knees. We felt pretty guilty, as they were meant for a surprise. We

The Reeves Eagle Mountain house, rebuilt

tried to put them back the way we found them, but Mom knew right away that we had found them. She put them away and we had to wait a long time before Mom let us have them, as a punishment for being snoopy.

As soon as the weather got better our parents started rebuilding a house. Sometimes some of the neighbors stopped to help.

An Unusual Childhood

The old burned house area was cleaned up, and everything, including the poor piano, was hauled away to a marshy place off in the timber. We searched the ashes, many times looking for Mom's diamond, but never found it.

One day while Daddy was working on the new house, Geraldine, Amy and Ruth Ellen came to play with us. They walked all the way. Daddy was working on the house and Ruth Ellen climbed up on the timbers overhead. She had our new cat, and she walked along till she was over our Dad's head and dropped the cat. It landed on Daddy's head and all four feet and clutching claws. He dropped his hammer and swore.

Ruth Ellen was laughing but she was afraid to come down right away. Finally Mrs. Parker came after her girls, Ruth Ellen, saw her walking down the lane, and yelled, "Look at our Moms walking like a duck". Mrs. P. was pregnant again and could hardly get about. Her children made fun of her constantly.

The Reeves family about 1921, from left, Dad Harley, Bud, the dog, Sylvia, Clyde, Harlene and Burley. Mom, Naomie, standing. This must be the new house after the other one burned.

We liked our new house, though it wasn't as big as the burnt one. It had a cellar underneath, and a bathroom. The only equipment in the bathroom was a huge tub on legs. It slanted at one end and we could soap it real slick and slide down, ker-splash into the water.

The kitchen had a sink with cold water. The water came from long pipes, running from far up Eagle Creek. It ran by

26

gravity to the cellar, and we could pump it by pitcher pump into the sink. Many times Sylv and I washed the dishes, but we hated doing the kettles and pans, so we would sneak them down in the cellar and set them up above the walls, with water in them, to soak. Mom would get to wondering where all her cooking ware was, and then we ended up washing all of the pans and kettles at once.

When the summer after the fire came, we were all scrubbed clean, put on our best clothes and a lunch made. Daddy had the buggy all polished and he even wore a tie. I remember staring at him; I had never seen him with a tie before. We all got seated and took off for Gardiner.

It seemed like some sort of holiday, the trees were fresh and green, new grass growing under the sagebrush, and even the sage had new color with their blooms. It was several hours to Gardiner and we had some good fights in the back seat of the buggy. Mom had Bud in front and she finally had to take Clyde up front too, because I and Burl kept teasing him.

When we got to Gardiner, we saw people everywhere. It seemed like the whole town was going the same way we were. We saw the Ritchies and the Scotts. Mr. Scott was a good friend of Daddy's. He went about in a wheel chair. Daddy drove the horses to a place where there were a lot of other horses and buggies. We all got down and went to a place where all the other people were going.

To our surprise, Mom and Daddy took Sylvia by the hand and went ahead; everyone was smiling at them and at us, too. There was a wooden stage, with benches on it and flags over head. Mom and Daddy told us to wait beside the stage, and to our surprise they took Bud and Sylv up the steps and on the stage, where everyone could see them. Everyone started clapping their hands and cheering.

There was a strange man there, he took Sylv by the hand and pulled her up front. Sylv was scared, she put her head down, and couldn't say a word. She looked quite small and thin, even with her best dress on. Her legs seemed awful skinny in her long black stockings. Everyone was very quiet.

An Unusual Childhood

The strange man, then told everyone how Sylv had saved Bud from the fire and made everyone cheer, although some of the ladies were crying. Then he took a box out of his pocket and opened it. It had a real gold medal in it. He bent down and pinned the medal on Sylv. Then he shook hands with Mom and Daddy, and he took Bud and held him up, so everyone could see that he was alive and well. There was more cheering and applause.

We waited till Mom and Daddy came down to us. Sylv was still afraid of all the people, a lot of them wanted to look at her and the medal. It was a gold Carnegie Hero Award, given to her for risking her life for saving Bud from the burning house.

This was a long, tiring day, and we were quiet and sleepy on the way home. As I write this, Sylv still has the medal; that was 49 years ago.

Summer was here again, Daddy was busy finishing our house and working in the Jardine mines. He came home on weekends, bringing the mail, groceries and candy.

There was a wide crack in the floor under the eaves, in the boys' room. We could line up there, lying on our stomachs, eating candy, and peering down into the kitchen at Mom and Daddy.

Mom did the farm work when Daddy was gone, we all had to help. The hay had to be mowed, and gardening done, we could pull weeds and were not too small to pile the windrowed hay into piles, called "shocks," to dry.

When Daddy came home, the hay was hauled to the barn and to a big stack in one of the fields. Our job was to ride on the wagon to tramp the piles of hay down as they were pitched up on the wagon. Usually we were bare-foot, and as there was an occasional thistle in the hay, we hated the task.

It was fun riding on the loaded wagon to the stacks, but here we got the tramp-down job on the stacks. The good alfalfa and timothy was stacked near the barn for the cows and work horses. The grass and wild hay was for the rest of the horses. Then there was a small field of oats for the hardworking horses.

While Daddy worked in Jardine, he worked in the evenings building a small log house for us to move into when school started. It had a lean-to bedroom, where we had our beds. Also, he built a small barn for a saddle horse and two cows, and a small hen house. This was our winter home and we hated it.

Here, for the first time, we met other boys and girls, and considered them stupid; no doubt we were stupid by their standards. Aunt Sadie and Uncle Dave were not our Aunt and Uncle. They were actually brother and sister, whose families were gone, so they lived on together. I don't know how Aunt Sadie's family had been lost to her, but Uncle Dave's family had drowned in a flash flood, and he had been unable to save them.

He and Aunt Sadie lived for a time in the little white Parker house that we had used. Aunt was lonely, she would often walk over to our house and, always, she brought goodies for us; sometimes cookies, cakes or homemade candy. She would tell us stories and we loved her.

Mom spent her time cooking, doing the washing and meeting more people than she had known before. We hated wash days; we would come home for lunch, and get bread and milk, as it took a lot of time over the washboard, and heating the boiler of water that was carried from Bear Creek.

We had fresh meat during the summer, whenever Mom or Daddy were lucky enough to kill a stubble-duck. Mom would can a lot of it. We had been warned not to tell anyone about the stubble-duck, as the rangers didn't want anyone shooting them.

Once, we had one in the kitchen, Mom was going to cook it and can it, but she had to go out for something; here came Aunt Sadie. She had a cake for us. We were so pleased that we went to the corner where the stubble-duck was hung behind a sheet, and showed Aunt Sadie the stubble-duck.

An Unusual Childhood

She was amazed, saying it looked a lot like a deer. When Mom came back, Aunt Sadie had gone, but we told Mom we had showed Aunt the stubble-duck, and Aunt Sadie had said it was a nice big one. Mom was shocked; she said we would probably all go to jail. No one ever came after us so I guess Aunt Sadie hadn't told the ranger.

Uncle Dave and Daddy decided to take tourists, called "dudes," into the mountains for sight-seeing and fishing. This was quite a project, saddle horses, pack horses and camp gear for two to three weeks at a time. Some of the "dudes" were eastern people from big cities and they were willing and able to pay.

My Dad said nearly all of them, at the end of the first all day horse back ride, wished they had never thought of it; but after that, they really enjoyed the fresh air, the quiet and good fishing. They saw a lot of wild country and passed through some old ghost towns. One of them, Solomon City, we were told, had board sidewalks and many houses yet standing. The windows were gone and some roofs fallen, there was tall grass and little trees growing where there were once streets. Another one was Independence, but it was mostly fallen, no doubt caved in by the heavy winter snows.

This was one of the most exciting and gratifying experiences the "dudes" encountered on their trips. There were a lot of wild animals to be seen--bear, elk, moose and deer. The coyotes made themselves heard but not seen; also plenty of squirrels and chipmunks. Now and then, in the evenings a wild scream from a cougar made the tethered horses snort in fear and I imagine the "dudes" felt a little shiver of fear.

When Daddy came back from these trips he had a lot to tell us about the people and excitement. One of these trips my Dad rode his favorite horse, Andy. During the day, a moose was seen. During the night, while everyone was sleeping soundly (after a camp meal, baked biscuits, cooked in a Dutch oven) there was a racket that woke everyone.

It was Andy. He had been hobbled so he could eat, but not stray too far. The moose, or a moose, had come close to camp, Andy had smelled the wild animal and tried to run; he fell over a log, and broke his leg. My Dad had to shoot him. Andy was his favorite horse.

One of the pack horses took Andy's place as a saddle horse; the pack was re-arranged on the other packs. We felt unhappy about Andy. I had ridden him, even though he was tall. We could lead him up by a stump; get on the stump then onto Andy's back. He was a spirited horse, tall and long-legged but slim. He was quiet and well-behaved when any of us kids got on him.

Early one morning, we heard a horse come galloping up to the house, and a man calling out to us. No one was up yet, but we got up and looked out the window; below was Jim Parker. Daddy went out to talk to him. Then Jim Parker rode away. We all rushed downstairs, and saw Mom crying. Daddy told us that Mrs. Parker had died, but she had 2 new baby girls.

Later, the funeral was held at the Parker house, and Mrs. Parker was buried between two big trees that grew along, out in the sage brush. Mr. Parker said she had often admired the big trees and mentioned how peaceful it was there. Mr. Parker made a white picket fence around the grave.

A short time later, one of the twin babies died and was buried beside her mother. Mr. Parker and the girls took care of the other baby. I don't remember her real name, but they called her "Jiggs.".

Later we noticed during the summer fly season, wild horses pushed the little white fence down and stood in the shade of the trees, right on top of the two graves. We never saw much of the Parker family after that.

Then the fall came and we had to move to Jardine, for school. We moved into the house that had been built, it was near Bear Creek—a river, actually. Across from the house and creek was a grove of timber. Above were the mills and mines. They were noisy, but we got used to them.

Our Dad went back to the ranch to take care of the horses and cows. We had to get up early to get the cows milked, and off to

An Unusual Childhood

the white school house up the hill. There were a lot of people in the town, a post office, small grocery store, two hotels, a boarding house, and just out of town, a fox farm, run by a Mrs. Morrison. She was quite wealthy and never was seen much in Jardine.

Burley, left, and Harlene headed to school.

We didn't mind school at first, but later were plenty tired of it. We missed the ranch, and when we went back on weekends, it was even harder to go to school. Some of the kids carried a lunch in a lard pail. At school we had a bucket of water in the school room with a dipper that everyone used. Later we had to bring our own drinking cups.

There were a lot of people who were from other countries; they formed little clans of their own. The school kids called then Dagos, and Wops. We were Hicks. One of our first days at school, Ruth Ellen Parker had made friends with another girl, leaving Sylv and I to ourselves. The other girl, Edna, had a lot of face powder on, so Ruth-Ellen tried it too. We told our folks about it, and decided we would call Edna "Powder Puff". The next day we walked behind Edna and called "Powder Puff". She didn't like it, so we started chanting "Powder Puff", and "Paint and Powder." Edna didn't do anything about it, so we made the most of it.

That evening, after school, Sylv and I were on our way home, when, out from behind a shed came several girls. They pounced on us. We were too surprised to do much, but they had both of us down in the dirt, and we sure got a beating. When they got through with us, we fled for home, our hair pulled, scratched, and bloody noses.

Harlene Jessie Reeves

Mom went to the school about it, but was told they couldn't do anything about it, and that we should learn to mind our own business. A bunch of the boys ganged up on Burl and chased him, throwing rocks. We told Daddy about it. He was quite angry and showed us how to fight. We got along fairly well after that. We found out that the miners' children had grown up in tough surroundings and knew how to fight.

Gradually we accepted the school routine. We made friends with the lady that ran a boarding house. We went by her house to and from school. She often gave us cake, left over from her meals. We didn't care if it was a day or two old, as we seemed to be hungry all the time. We sold milk to this same lady.

Then the snow came, we didn't see our Dad as often, as it was hard for horses to get through the snow. Sylv and I each got new woolly dresses, mine a blue stripe, and Sylvia's brown stripe. Mom somehow got the idea that I should always wear blue, and Sylvia should wear brown. We all wore long john underwear. The legs of them would get wider at the ankle, and we had to fold over the extra width and then put on the long black stockings. We always had a lump on our ankles, where the underwear was folded. It was all right though, as all the girls had lumpy ankles, for the same reason.

As the snow deepened, the hill to the school became almost impossible to climb, mainly because everyone brought out their sled, and packed the snow down by so many sledding down hill. We didn't have a sled. Burl made one of boards, it looked pretty good. The first time he tried it down the hill, it flattened out. He had forgotten to put braces under it. We wished for a "Flexible Flyer" a sled that could be steered, and was a little higher off the ground than the others.

All the grades from one to eight were in the same room and with one teacher, who lived in a little house near the school. Some of the big boys carried wood in to the teacher's desk. The bigger students sat toward the back of the room, and the little ones in front, we had double desks and seats, so two people could sit together. Every desk had a hole in it, for the ink bottle to sit in. Many girls had their long braids or curls, dipped in the inkwell by the boy who sat behind them.

An Unusual Childhood

At Christmas, some of the men brought a huge tree to the school. We were put to work, making paper chains, red and green. Each of us was given a "piece" to learn for the Christmas program. The whole town usually came to the program, as there was little other entertainment. Names were exchanged, and we each got a gift, usually homemade, but the Mining Company produced candy, apples and once, a gift for each child.

I still remember walking to the school house, the cold snow creaking under foot, and all of us singing "Silent Night". Everyone had to walk, and the groups were singing on their way.

The school room was opened, and it seemed different, the seats and desks pushed back to make room for the show. The room was warm and smelled of the green tree, covered with the twinkling candles. After everyone had said his "piece," Santa Claus would appear, and call out the names of the kids present, and each one got to go up and get his present. I was real lucky once, I got a play washboard. After Christmas we went back to the ranch for awhile.

It was good to get home, my Dad was a good cook, and had stew, piles of dried apple and apricots and the luxury of canned milk. There were the same old jobs of feeding the animals and cleaning the barn where the cows were kept. It was warm in the barn, with the cows living there, and it smelled like summer up in the hay overhead.

Also, the cats had moved into the barn. Any cat that was foolish enough to go straying was caught by the ever-hungry coyotes. At night, it was good to hear the wailing of the coyotes, and to snuggle deeper into the covers.

Then it was back to Jardine and school again, with spring a long way off. January was always extra cold. Our bunk beds had plenty of quilts, but no heater, so we slept completely covered, except for our noses and in the morning there were ice crystals in our nostrils. We would leap out of bed in the mornings and hurry into the main house, and get our clothes on as fast as possible by the heater.

Bud was lucky, he didn't have to go to school yet, but he got lonely. His bed was a huge trunk that we moved all our clothes in. It was fixed up with a mattress, and covers, and with the lid back, it made a dandy little bed. It was in the main room of the house were it wasn't so cold.

Finally, the great day came and school was out. Spring came, snow was melting away. There were little creeks running everywhere and the water raised in Bear Creek and ran over the timber area. There were ponds of melted snow and the boys seemed to think it was summer, they never went around the water, but walked right through it. When we got our report cards, telling us if we passed or not, we packed up and Daddy came for us with the wagon and we went home!

It took awhile for us to quiet down. There was so much to check up on, our old special places, the new calves and colts, and the dog. The elk herd moved across Casey's ranch, leaving trampled sagebrush and an odor of elk. It seemed like thousands of them, to us. The horses shed their long hair, and we found lots of wood ticks on them, some as big as grapes, they had been fastened on so long. As we got older, we wandered farther during the summer. We went to Casey's Lake, a small pond with almost an entire cover of water lilies.

There were two places way out in the middle that never had lilies, evidently deep holes. Much of this country was volcanic, and we believed the bare spots in the lake were former lava tubes. We never ventured very far out in the lake, mainly because we considered it unsafe, but did manage to get a few lilies. After coming out of the water we had to pull leeches off our legs. These were black, worm looking things that fastened themselves on our skin, sucking blood. They were discouraging; we never really enjoyed wading in Casey's Lake.

Sometimes we went up Eagle Creek to the old mill. The mill itself was gone, but a lot of the boards, timbers and junk lumber were thrown every which way across the creek. We could run along the boards and jump over the empty places to other boards. The creek was underneath, and could be seen through places the lumber didn't cover. Our Dad used a lot of this lumber, though it had to be sorted, since a lot of it was getting rotten.

An Unusual Childhood

We dragged some of the better slats out and made stilts for ourselves; also we staked out claims, using old lumber, and laying out the frames of our houses. If we had been asked to carry that much wood in for the stoves, it would have been a dreadful job, but we carried loads of it for our pretend homes.

We found a mud hole in the cow pasture, it wasn't very big, but after we kept wading through it, it got bigger and deeper. Sylv was the only one who wouldn't wade it. She was being a lady.

One day we got a lot of baling wire, and a big wooden box. We tied the wire to all four corners of the box, and managed to climb a big tree, and get the wire over a thick branch. It made a fine swing, we all used it, to try it out, not realizing that the wire was breaking as it was moved back and forth.

Sylv decided it looked good, so she went up the tree, out of the limb and into the box, she didn't get to swing much though, the wires broke and dumped her, box and all. She hurt her back, but as all ailments, it was considered a passing injury and allowed to heal itself.

When the summer rains came, they were sudden and violent with thunder and lighting. We stayed away from big trees, and tried to be at home when they struck. It was one thing we were very respectful of, as we saw the split and burned trees that the lightening had done.

One summer we were going to brave it out, we got a tarp and all of us got under it, out in the yard. The thunder was all about us, and lightening striking in several directions at once. Then the rain came with a roar, down on our tarp. We were scared silly, but not silly enough to get out and run for the house. After it was over, we crawled out and were sort of quiet for awhile. After that, we tried to be near home when the black clouds began gathering over Grey Donkey.

After a bad storm, the air was fresh and cool, the robins in the cow pasture trees went mad with song. The chickens went on walkabout, their feathers soaked and bedraggled. I avoided them;

they were more stupid looking than when dry. I never liked chickens since my cousin, Virginia, chased me around with a feather duster. At first it was fun, but she kept running at me, hitting with those feathers till I got panicky, I even hit her in the face with a wet dish-rag; we finally were pulled apart by Mom and Aunt Rene.

As we grew older, we went farther from home, we explored the horse pasture, and their corral. There was a cold spring there, and a long wooden trough, that the icy water ran in. We often stayed for a cold drink and to lick the horses' salt block. There were some big Aspen trees here that we climbed. Once we found a robin's nest, with the beautiful robins blue eggs. We took them home, and Mom made us take them back. It didn't do any good; the mother robin left her nest and never came back.

The horse pasture had several trails the horses made, when they came to drink at the corral; on one of these trails was some old clothing, faded and rotten, walked over by horses, and weather ruined.

Sylv told us that a cow puncher had died there, and that was all that was left of him. I wasn't a bit in sympathy of this poor pitiful sight, because I thought a cow puncher was a mean person who went around with a long sharp stick, punching the poor cows. It served him right to die on the trail.

Sylv could keep us spellbound with her knowledge. During the summer, the cattle were turned out on the range. Some of the cows wore bells, so we could hear them and find them easier. It was because our task was to go after the milk cows in the evenings. They were locked in a pen overnight, and turned out after milking in the morning.

Sometimes we waited too long before going after the cows, and it got dark. The cows would bed down and we had to be alert to hear a bell, when one of them moved. Often the cows drifted up past Porcupine Jim, a hill; it was a long way, especially after it was dark.

We learned to not be afraid of the dark. A big black bear would loom up in front of us, and when we ran at it and yelled, it

An Unusual Childhood

would turn out to be a stump. When we finally found the cows, they would gladly rise, and run for home. They never thought about coming home by themselves. We had a young white faced bull, we trained him to ride, and one of us, the lucky one, could get a ride home on the bull. The only problem was that he would go through brush and try to scrape the rider off against the trees.

One of the cows was mean. She would run home with the rest of them, but in the corral, she would lower her head and chase everyone out of the corral. One day I climbed down the fence into the corral, and let her see me. I had a big club in my hands. She ran at me and at the last minute, I hit her across the face with the club. She was cured of her bad habit then.

Then we had Old Holiday, a milk cow. She was gentle and gave lots of milk. Once, when we couldn't find her with the others, we gave up, and brought the others in. The next morning, here came Holiday, escorting a shiny new calf. It was exciting, as we knew a cow had nothing to do with Sears Roebuck.

We loved to wander up Eagle Creek, and had berry picking expeditions. We found lots of obsidian arrow heads, but never saved them, they were so common. Also, there were lots of snail shells that the snail had moved out of. This whole country had silver and gold deposits, and we often picked up pieces of gold bearing ore, the veins of gold clearly standing out. Our Dad had a piece of ore with a gold nugget the size of a pea sticking out of it.

There were several working mines in Jardine, and plenty of abandoned holes. One shaft was straight down; I don't know how the former miners worked it. We used to lie on our stomachs and yell down the hole, and drop rocks down. It was so deep, we could drop a rock, and wait awhile before we heard it hit bottom. It was big enough for a horse to fall in, I don't know why a Reeves kid didn't fall it, or the rim break and several Reeves kids disappear. Luck seemed to be with us on most of our projects.

In Jardine, there was an abandoned mine in a hillside. We went by it on our way to school. On our way home one day we decided to explore it. The wooden supports were rotten and several had fallen, but we climbed over them, and on and on we went. It was totally dark and we felt our way along the walls, stepping ahead carefully, in case there was a down shaft. We went until we met a branch, going two different ways. Here we stopped as we were afraid we couldn't find our way back if we made a turn. Then we started screaming and yelling, the echoes would go back and forth and fade away under the mountain.

After tiring of this sport, we made our slow way back out of the mine, climbing over any old fallen rocks and rotting timbers. When we finally could see daylight ahead, we, or at least I, suddenly felt afraid of that echoing darkness behind us and scrambled out in a hurry. We never told our folks about this, just in case they wouldn't like it. In later years, we told our parents some of these things we did, and they were quite shocked.

As we grew older, we were allowed to ride horses, and we each had our own horse. Sylv's was Toots. She was a pretty bright sorrel color, with four white stockings and a white blaze in her face. Sylv named her Glorianna, also Flossie, and Joyce; but she was called Toots. Mom liked Toots especially too. She trained her to kneel and a few other horse tricks. Mom rode her in a Parade in Gardiner, and

Bud and Harlene on horseback, 1926.

the mare loved it. She even danced in time with the bands, and made a great hit with the people.

Then there was Rock. Rock was the color of an old grey rock, and almost as fast moving. Clyde got to ride him, usually. Rock did something to Clyde's love of horses, he hates them even today.

My horse was a red roan, Dot. She was one of the fastest horses we owned. Then there was Paint, a small pinto with a bad front knee. I don't know which of the boys claimed Paint but he was a favorite. We could all ride him the same time if we wished. Then someone had to ride Lady, with the wide back, or Pat, a red roan who had seen better times, but was dependable. I never liked Pat too well, because he and Dot always stood around together and I thought Dot could find a prettier companion.

Dot got tangled in some barb wire and cut her front foot through the hoof and to the bone. Mom kept her tied in a clean grassy area, and washed the cut with salt water, after that, she put wads of bag balm on it. It seemed to get worse, and since my Dad was gone, Mom was plenty worried.

One day the ranger came by. He stopped to see if we had any dead deer on our faces, so Mom asked him to look at Dot's foot and what we should do. He didn't have many ideas. However, he took his revolver out of his holster and offered to Mom. Wow! She got mad. The ranger left. He was no match against Mom, even if he did have a gun.

Dot didn't do much work that summer, but she did start healing up and finally was as good as new, except for the thickened hoof.

When fall came, the Aspens and Cottonwoods turned yellow and flaming red. Lots of the berry bushes turned color and the big spruce's and pines seemed darker and greener with the bright leaves.

Mom would get a lot of material from Sears Roebuck and start fall sewing. Our new long johns came in the mail, fuzzy and warm and nice fitting tight legs. Then there were shoes, sometimes new jackets, and mittens. Mom usually made the boys caps.

Then we had to pack up and go back to Jardine. We had made friends there by now, so it wasn't so bad. We had a new teacher. Her daughter, Cecilia, was in Sylv's and my class. She was quite pretty, with long dark curls, and snobbish, since her Mom was the teacher. One day at recess, I got into a fight with her and she started pulling my hair, so I got two hands full of her long curls and wouldn't let go.

Cecilia was screaming for her mother, so she came out, pushed the ring of spectators apart and got us apart. She told me to go home, which I was glad to do, but when I got home, Mom wasn't a bit happy to see me come home so early. She got a stick and marched me all the way back, not caring for my embarrassments.

She and the teacher tried to talk the problem over, and teacher said something that made Mom mad, it looked like there was going to be another hair pulling match, and Mom finally went home, leaving me at school.

Classes went on as thought nothing had happened. Cecelia was kept indoors after the fight. Teacher left that spring and we had a new teacher the next year. Sylv made friends with Edna, so I tried to be friendly with Edna's younger sister, Edith. Edith was much prettier than Edna; she had long curls, but no friends. I found out she didn't care if she had friends or not, she was a pretty face with nothing behind it. We would have called her retarded today.

There were several characters in the town, probably more than average for a town that size. There was "Bobbie" who worked as a miner. He was, small and had an odd voice. All the wives were somewhat shook up when Bobbie got sick, and during his ailment, it was discovered that Bobbie was a woman. He—or she—left town soon after.

Then there was old Webster, a complete alcoholic. He came to our house once. We and Mom were alone. He pounded on the door, Mom opened it and Webster fell in. He managed to get to his

An Unusual Childhood

feet, so Mom told him to get out. He didn't want to get out and put up an argument. He said "I knew you when you were poor." We thought we were still poor.

He continued his argument, leaning off to the North West, finally fell and couldn't get up. He was prepared to sleep, but Mom got him by the heels and Sylv held the door open, and Mom dragged old Webster out. The door was closed and we were rid of Webster. Later on he drank himself into a stupor, and fell down, no one came by, and as he was outdoors, he froze to death. I've never had much faith in alcohol as an anti-freeze after poor old Webster's death.

Then there was Johnny K., who was insane. He lived with his widowed mother, who was a tiny, shriveled old lady. Johnny was considered harmless, but he acted like a child of two or so. He was a big, handsome man but his little mother had to spoon feed him.

He was her whole life, no one cared to visit her as it excited Johnny and he became un-manageable. He loved to stay out on the front porch and yell, "Hi" to anyone who passed by. He would pound the rail with his fists until his hands were sore. His mother would place pillows on the porch rail, to keep Johnny's hands from getting hurt, but he would knock the pillows off, and keep on beating the railing. We were terribly afraid of Johnny.

Then there was Jack Rose. He was part-time miner, fur trapper and probably moon shiner. He had dogs. He was a bachelor, lived in a tiny cabin, with his dogs, their harness, his saddle, wood box, bunk and camp gear. It was a fascinating place.

The arsenic-eater was a strange man. He tried over and over to commit suicide by eating arsenic. Arsenic was easy to come by; it was heaped in a huge pile near the stamping mill. It seemed that the arsenic became acceptable to his body, and he would get sick, and recover. Many of the men tried to persuade him not to eat the stuff, but he would get some again. The rumor would go over town that the arsenic-eater was sick again. Poor man, he didn't want to live, but was afraid to die.

Then arrived an old Scotchman, our Dad hired him to help

with the chores during the winter. This man was frugal to a ridiculous point. He never threw a scrap of food away. He cooked oatmeal by spreading it in a pan and browning it in the oven. He would lick his spoon until he practically wore the finish off. He always would say to us, "It's good for your stomach," no matter if it was a cold dry biscuit, or a dish of oatmeal.

He wasn't a very big man but as winter came on, be began adding more and more clothes, until he looked like a walking rag bag. When my Dad left him to feed our animals one winter, he nearly starved our dog to death, as he didn't want to waste food on an animal yet he had saved some old biscuits up in the cupboard till they were hard as rocks. Then, instead of feeding our work horses their regular oats, he had snooped around and found a dab of oats, put away on a high shelf in the kitchen.

This, he thought wasteful, so fed them to our team. He led them to water afterward, one of them didn't want to drink, but the other did, and immediately fell dead. It seemed that he had fed our poisoned gopher oats to the horses. He left in a hurry, and we were glad, as that "good for your stomach" went with every meal when he was with us.

There was a lady who lived alone in town; she never had our mothers go to visit. In fact, if Mom and some of the other ladies were talking about her, they always stopped talking if any of us came near. It made us curious, so one day, after spying her house; we got up our nerve and knocked on her door. We felt like running when we heard her coming to the door. She opened the door.

"Yes" she asked.

We got a feeling to giggle, but one of the boys said "We came to visit you." She remarked how nice that was as she was lonely and was hoping someone would come.

She treated us just like we were grown-up. We went in and stared about the room. There was a beaded curtain, between the kitchen and living room. The curtains were bright red with lots of ruffles. She had fancy lamps sitting about; they had bright colored shades, with ribbon bows. There were Kewpie dolls on shelves and tables, with huge colored feather fans behind them. Our hostess opened several boxes of chocolates and we ate all we wanted. She seemed to have plenty of chocolates.

She was quite beautiful to our eyes. Her hair was a brilliant red, very curly and piled up on her head. Her cheeks and lips were unusually red and she smelled like flowers. Her dress was of silk, and it was red, too, with lots of ruffles and lace and very low in front, but she had beads around her neck. She was really nice to us, asking our names and all about school, and kept giving us more chocolates.

I sort of hoped she would give me on of the Kewpie dolls. I could tear the feathers off its behind, and it would be a pretty nice doll. I didn't ask though, because our parents had told us not to ask for anything. Finally our hostess told us we should go, as she had some work to do, and we took some more candy and left.

At supper that night, we told our parents about our visit and how nice that lady was. To our surprise, Mom and Daddy got mad and said if we ever went near her again, they would wear the razor strap out on us. They always meant what they said, so after that we turned our heads the other way when we passed her house, even if she waved to us from her window. We felt quite foolish not to wave back, but she didn't wave at us anymore.

Among other strange people there was Joe Tripple, a recluse who lived out of Jardine, up Bear Creek. I don't know how he lived, as he seldom came to town, but he also hoped to strike it rich, so he could send for his family "in the old country." I don't think anyone went near him; he must have been terribly lonely.

We had a neighbor family that we liked; anyway; we liked Mary M., the mother. She had a son Ray, about Burl's age, and a smaller boy, Roy, also a baby girl, Phoebe. Mary's husband had run away and left her so she got a divorce. Our parents had taken Mary to Livingston to get the divorce, as they didn't sell them in Jardine or Gardiner.

Mary M. was terribly overweight, but good-natured. Phoebe

Harlene Jessie Reeves

was chubby too, Sylv loved to carry her about and play with her, but we found Jack Rose's dogs more interesting, especially the one who got sick and lay dying for about a week behind the cook stove. Poor dog, he might have recovered if Jack R. had not tried out so many cures on him.

Mary's boy, Ray, went to school, but his little brother didn't. So when their aunt, Laura R. and her husband went back in the mountains to trap for a long time, they took Roy with them. That way, Mary M. could work as a cook, she had only little Phoebe to look after, Ray was big enough to look after himself.

Sylv took care of Phoebe after school. I got plenty tired of Phoebe, it seemed every time I wanted Sylv to play with me she had that doggone baby on her back.

After about a long summer in the mountains, Laura R. and her husband came back to Jardine. Ray M. came to our house to tell us that his little brother, Roy, was home. We all ran down to see him, as things had been pretty dull.

When we came into the house, Roy darted on all fours, behind the cook stove. From that safe corner, he growled and barked at us. We hadn't realized that he had been with dogs for so long that instead of talking, he reacted like a dog at the sight of strangers. It took a while for Roy to join the human race.

Among the younger set were the new kids. They were three small sisters; they were immediately branded as "Wops", and given the exclusion treatment. Actually they were pretty little girls, clean to the point of being polished, their silvery white-blonde hair pig-tailed so tightly it must have hurt. They were dressed alike, with neat little aprons and a hanky in the apron pockets. They seemed to constantly be using their hankies for their noses (instead of their sleeves) and for lunch wipe-ups. All three were placed in the front row, where we could all look at them.

They snuggled together like frightened kittens, not making a sound even when the bigger boys shot them with spit wads. The pay-off came when the smallest sister had to go to the toilet, and was to

45

An Unusual Childhood

frightened to ask permission to leave. She finally lost control, and not only filled the seat and wet down her sisters clothes but it ran over on the floor and down the aisle. Her sisters leaped up like fluttery matrons, their hankies fairly flew, as they tried to mop up the damage.

We didn't get to see all as the teacher told everyone to go outdoors for awhile. We were sorry for these girls, as it had not been too long since we had been strangers like them. The three continued in school, but never seemed to make friends. Finally they passed word around that there was going to be a party at their house.

It was on a Wednesday evening, we Reeves kids were on hand, but no one else came. The father made us welcome, though we could hardly understand his strange accent. The three sisters were so shy the evening was ruined, but we did eat a lot of boxed chocolates. The party was probably an attempt by the parents to make their little girls accepted, but it didn't work. They moved away soon after that.

Then there was the horrible Lester. He had a stupid round face, covered with freckles, and mouse colored hair. He was so silly that all the boys liked him. He had a dumb habit of saying "Tickeeee-." One terrible day, all the boys and some of the girls had dared Lester to kiss me. I didn't know it, but the whole school was alerted—even my own brothers, and probably Sylv. I had gone behind the big map of the world, (it was on an easel sort of thing) and was looking up something, when Lester slunk up behind me and kissed me on the back of my neck.

I believe that only the teacher was ignorant of what happened. Everyone was laughing, Lester was "Tickeee-ing" and I was out the door and running for home. I scrubbed my neck, and bawled, but Mom made me go back to school and face all the snickers.

I went home another time, this time I had my feelings hurt. There were two out houses, besides the school, one for girls and the other for the boys. One of the lowest forms of little boys went in the girls' toilet, and did his job on the floor. The teacher was furious; she let the boys go outdoors and asked for the guilty party to confess. No one volunteered, so one of the big girls told the teacher I had done it.

46

Harlene Jessie Reeves

I can still see her, Rosetta by name, staring at me with her big blue eyes and accusing me! I don't know why she disliked me; perhaps I had stared at her, as I thought she was the most beautiful girl I had ever seen. I left, running for home again, even as the teacher yelled at me to stop.

This time my Mom accompanied me back to school, there was quite a battle, until, Rosetta, with a red face admitted that she knew who was really guilty and she went home crying. She hated me ever after.

We made friends with the Jones family. Their father worked in the mines too; they had two boys and two girls. We liked Earl, the younger boy and the girls, Helen and Ruby, but hated Ray the older boy. He had a filthy mind and was to be avoided. Mrs. Jones and Mom became friends, and we sometimes ate at each others house.

The fall was a nice season, we hated to be shut up in school and miss the Indian summer, with the colorful trees and warm sunny days. The nights began to get cold, and frost appeared. During the first snow, the hunters began to arrive from all over the nation. Their goal was elk. Elk were moving down from the higher mountains and from Yellowstone Park.

The opening day of hunting sounded like a second battle of Little Big Horn. The hunters stationed themselves before dawn around the area of Buffalo Flats and waited. The elk usually migrated in big herds, coming across the border of Yellowstone Park. There they met a bombardment from all sides. There were a lot of arguments as to which animal belonged to which hunter. Sometimes a hunter was wounded and once in a while a man was killed.

After the season was over, the town became quiet, and the snow fell daily. It got so deep we could make tunnels to our play snow houses. After a hard freeze, we could walk every where on top the snow. We had one cow to milk; it was cold in the barn so we dreaded that chore. We had a half-grown kitten. He loved to sit by the milk stool and was adept at drinking the warm milk we squirted in his face.

An Unusual Childhood

One morning he made a bad mistake, after eating the milk, he walked over and sat down on a piece of tin and began to lick his paws to wash his face. When he put his dampened paws down on the cold tin, he stuck to the tin, frozen to it. I pulled him off and he howled in pain as the skin stayed on the frozen tin. It took him some time to recover, but he never sat on a piece of tin again.

We burned a lot of wood during the winter, Daddy had hauled a lot of logs up by the house in the fall and we had a long cross cut saw. That was a daily job for two of us to use. When it was cut in blocks, part of them had to be split for the cook stove. Then it was stacked on the porch, to keep dry. Every evening after school, we had the sawing, splitting stacking job, or freeze.

There were a lot of dogs around town, so we were inspired to get a dog team. We had all kinds, big and little, belonging to the neighbors. We got clothes line rope and wire, from which we made dog harness to fit each dog. It was quite a problem, the dogs were not cooperating, but we finally got them lined up, and by having someone in front to lead, we got the dogs trained to run. They would go along fine until one dog would nip another; and there would be a big dog fight, tangling and tearing up our long harness job.

It kept us busy many Saturdays, and no doubt furnished a laugh to the people who saw the strange assortment of dogs go by. The weather would get to 30 degrees below, but didn't seem cold. The folks each got an elk for our winter meat. Instead of a locker, the meat was hung outdoors, out of reach of dogs, and wrapped in a sheet, so the birds couldn't get it.

Mom had a platform out side the kitchen window; she put suet and crumbs out on it. The birds flocked to it, the little busy chickadees, and camp-robbers. They were beautiful with their grey and blue coloring and became quite tame.

Once, Mom put an old bird cage on the platform. She left its door open, and tied a string to the door, and under the window frame. When a camp robber went in to eat, Mom pulled the string, and closed the door and we owned a camp robber! Later on Mom turned him loose because he got so hysterical.

Harlene Jessie Reeves

School went on and on. There wasn't much excitement, but once Sylv decided she would be more grown up if she wore Moms corset to school. The corset was a vicious arrangement of cloth, whalebone and long strings. It fit Sylv from under her arms down over her hips. She was thin, so I had to pull the strings as far as they would go and tie them. There was a lot of ties left hanging, but we fixed them in big hoops so they wouldn't hand below her dress hem. It was OK until we had to sit for a long time.

Sylv and I sat at the same desk so after lunch Sylv wanted me to change places with her so I sat next to the wall, Sylv on the aisle, next to the other kids. She whispered to me that she couldn't stand the corset any longer, it was so stiff that she couldn't bend to sit, but had to slide her feet ahead and sit on the edge of the seat, about like making a board sit down. So I sat sideways, cutting off the view of the other students, while Sylv maneuvered the corset off, a little at a time.

It took quite a while as she had to untie strings and loosen the thing until it would slide off. When it was loose, Sylv slid out of it like a snake shedding its skin. It was a problem getting her feet up on the seat and pulling the corset off, without attracting attention. If the teacher noticed her, she probably thought Sylv was itching. Finally the thing was off, and Sylv very quietly rolled it up and shoved it in the desk, out of sight. All this was done without pulling her dress up.

As school went on, we got to buy new books. Each of us was allowed to order a library book. I ordered a book, "Black Beauty". I liked horse stories the most. By the time each student had ordered his favorite, we had a well-assorted library.

Then the state sent free iodine tablets, as there was a shortage of iodine in Montana. We also got free samples of Mentholatum. At home we cut out and sent away for free samples of all sorts of things. The one I remember most was Ovaltine.

One winter I sold Cloverine Salve and got a doll for my-self. It wasn't as nice as its picture in the magazine. We all wanted skis, many people had them. Our parents made a pair. They got the boards, and cut them in shape. Then they were thinned and painted.

An Unusual Childhood

After that the boards were soaked--the tip ends anyway. The water they were soaked in was hot. Then the tip ends were pushed between the ceiling rafters and a weight hung on the other ends to force the tips to bend. This process went on for a long time; we ate our meals with this ski apparatus hanging over our table. I don't recall if these boards ever became skis, I presume they did, as their presence was finally removed from our table.

Winter wore on; our underwear lost its fuzziness and got baggy at the ankles again. We got tired of being indoors and found lots to do. Some of the people left because the mines slowed down, due to less profitable ore.

We picked up many cast-off miner caps, each with its little carbide lamp attached to the front. These lamps were all the light the miners had, as there was no electricity in the town yet. Carbide is a smelly grey powder, when it contacts water, it bursts into flame.

The miners had the lamps attached to their caps, a handy light that glowed just ahead of them as they worked in the blackness of the mine. We accumulated our own little supply of carbide from old caps; we could dump it beside some water and let it burn, like magic.

We had a dog, Fanny, who was a mixture of collie and shepherd. She was a nice dog, worked in our shed team and went everywhere we went. One day our Dad locked her in the un-used chicken house, telling us to keep her there. We didn't know why she was jailed and felt sorry for her. Her friends came to see her and tried to get in. We chased them away, except for one dog that belonged to Jack Rose. We let him in to visit Fanny. Then he wouldn't get out, so we shut him up too, and ran off, not wanting Daddy to know we had opened the chicken house.

When Daddy found the two dogs locked up, instead of one-- he was surprised. He was mad at us; then he and Mom started laughing at how clever Jack Rose's dog was, and we didn't tell how he got in. Anyway, they decided to let Fanny out. Jack R. told us he wasn't mad at us for locking his dog up, he just laughed about it.

Harlene Jessie Reeves

Spring was coming again; Mom sent to Sears Roebuck and got material for spring dresses. Mine was blue dotted voile and Sylv's was brown dotted voile. Mom got each of us a straw hat, with ribbons and artificial cherries on them; we didn't get to wear them much as there was no special place to go. Some of the mothers went for walks and visited each other, all dressed up.

Usually our brothers didn't want to go visiting, but once Mom and Sylv and I went to see a lady who had a new baby. She also had two little girls; the older one was Dorothy, and the other one bawled most of the time. This lady had freckles all over, and when she opened her dress to nurse the baby, I was shocked to see she had freckles there too.

Clyde had come with us, and when we left, Mom had to find Clyde. He and Dorothy had gone snooping in their Dad's woodshed and found a batch of beer. This was home made brew, and Dorothy and Clyde had drunk enough that both of them were staggering. We never went visiting there again.

Gradually, spring came again, the sky was blue-green and new grass came up. Sylv and I and Edna put on an outdoor play, we had long fancy dresses, made of old curtains and what-ever else we could find. We made up a table of fairies and mountain princesses. We strung blankets between trees, on a little grassy place, and sent out word all over town, about the play.

We had an audience of three or four mothers, who didn't want to pay the 5 cent admission, so we cut it to 1 cent. There were several little kids and our mothers. The play came apart, our curtain fell down and we all wanted to be the star. It was fun, and everyone sat around talking till it was time to go home and cook their suppers.

We all passed our grades and school was out. Off to the ranch again. Actually we had more work to do at the ranch than in Jardine, but most of the work was outdoors and we liked it. We were allowed to ride horses when we went after the cows, but sometimes, the horses were out in the pasture and it was just as easy to walk, as to go after a saddle horse.

An Unusual Childhood

When the ranch work was caught up, Daddy moved his camp gear back up in the mountains, to work on the ditch. Everything went as usual at home; we had more chores, and learned how to drive a team.

Five Reeves kids in a tree - can you see them? One is hanging upside down.

Our Dad had cleared more sage brush and it had to be burned. The sagebrush was cut off at the roots with a mattock. It was hard work, but the new fields were planted to oats the first year. There was the garden and potato field, also the strawberries. The hillside cellar had to be cleared of the old sprouting vegetables.

Some people came up from Gardiner. They were young people, looking for a good picnic spot. We were awed by their shiny buggy and matched team. Mom told them to drive on up Eagle Creek to a crossing above the old mill, where there was a small but sunny meadow. I believe we were there before the picnickers. We were hidden, of course. They spread a blanket, and got baskets of goodies out of their buggy. They did a lot of silly talking and giggling, and their team was un-hitched and tied away from the picnic spot, so the flies would leave the food alone.

We were as still as fawns in our hiding places. Finally one of the young men pointed at our hideaway and said, "All right, you can come out now." We were afraid they would be mad, but they gave each of us a purple plum—the first we had ever seen. They made us promise to go home, so we did, even though we thought of hiding in a different place and continue watching the proceedings.

Mom was on the way to the picnic grounds, she had Bud with her, and when we met her she said she should give all of us a good whipping. We thought she was going up to watch the picnic too, but she went home with us.

During that summer, Mom took one of our "green" broke horses and rode up in the horse pasture, to see if the fences were all right and to find the horses and check up on them.

Harlene Jessie Reeves

On her way home, her horse didn't want to come back; he fought his bit and tried to buck. Going down a hill, Mom was leaning forward when the horse threw his head back, hitting Mom in the face with his bony horse head. It nearly knocked her out, but she managed to get him home and put the horse in the corral.

She came to the house, and we were shocked to see her. Her nose was swollen and both eyes blackened. She said her neck hurt and felt like it was broken. She wasn't hungry and went to bed. The next day, Mom felt even worse, and said one of us would have to go get Daddy. Sylv had to stay and look after Mom, Burl and Clyde were too young, so it was decided that I would go.

Mom said to take Paint, he had been on that trail many times, and wouldn't run away, he was slow but dependable. So I started out, feeling very important, I hadn't been on that trail very many times. It was fine as far as Parkers; I even hoped they would see me, all by myself, on an important mission.

Paint knew the way and there was no problem there. As we left Parkers fence line, I began to get scared. We crossed the marshy spot with its fallen trees, and there was dead silence, except for the creaking saddle and Paints footsteps.

It was a nice sunny day, but I was cold with fear. I tried to whistle, but stopped in case something might hear me. Finally the worst part up the trail was ahead, the tall timber. I desperately wanted to turn back. This timber was dark and gloomy even at noonday, the trees tall and close together, the trail wound here and there over fallen logs and around thick clumps. The only sound was an occasional "lost" sound as a bit of wind blew through the tree tops, and the sad call of the "Phoebe" bird as it seemed to move along somewhere ahead of us.

Even Paint became alert, lifting his head and his ears forward. Finally we came to some occasionally sunny spots, where the trees thinned out and into an area of Christmas trees. We called them by that name, as they were young, green, thick trees, with candle-appearing new growth on their branches.

53

An Unusual Childhood

It wasn't far to my Dad's camp, and I rode in, full of importance, fear left behind. His horse neighed, so I couldn't surprise Daddy. He came out of his tent, where he was just cooking lunch. I gave my message, so Daddy closed the camp stove, to kill the fire, he gave me some cold biscuits, and saddled his horse, and we headed for home. I got so tired by the time we reached Parkers I could hardly stay on my horse. Paint was tired, too, his bad knee causing him to limp and stumble.

Daddy was in a great rush to get home, we were left far behind, so Paint and I almost made the trip back alone. It wasn't so

Harley fishing in one of the Montana mountain lakes.

scary, though, we were not far behind. Mom was glad to have Daddy home. He started putting clothes, wrung in hot water, on her neck, which made her feel better, but she had to stay in bed a long time. We had to do more work when Daddy was in charge, and he showed Sylv and I how to cook. Then it was our job.

Daddy was worried about his camp, which he had left so hurriedly, as a bear had been hanging around it. Finally Mom was able to be up, but couldn't do much because of her neck aching. She had some of us rubbing her neck when she was tired. It was quite a while before she rode a horse again.

54

Harlene Jessie Reeves

One day that summer, we went up the lane to the garden, and across the big field, we saw a strange brown object. It was on the road that went from Parker's to Gardiner. We retreated to our lane, and got behind some trees, which gave us a view, so we could watch whatever the brown thing was.

We could see that it was moving very slowly along the road. As we had never seen such a thing before, we ran for home, and reported it to Daddy. He decided to go see for himself, we tagged along behind, just in case the strange critter was getting nearer.

Daddy came back and to our questions he said he wasn't sure, but it looked like a Rhinoceros. After a while Uncle Dave came along, of course he had to pass the strange animal to get to our place so we asked him if he had seen it. He was surprised, said he hadn't seen anything on the road, in fact he had been on the road for some time. He had been raking the loose rocks off the road all morning. Only then did we realize that Uncle Dave in a brown overcoat was the slow moving bent-over critter on the road.

We should have learned by this time that our Dad liked to tease us, and he looked so solemn, we couldn't tell the difference. They (Uncle Dave and Daddy) were great friends. When the most work was caught up, Uncle Dave came and asked Daddy to go with him again, with a group of "dudes," both of the men were good camp cooks, and could take care of a lot of riders, horses and camps. This time Geraldine Parker and a boy friend went along too. My Dad didn't like it, as she made fun of the "dudes," and told wild stories to them.

She told them to watch closely on the mountain sides, as they might catch a glimpse of a goatafrow. They kept watching and asking about the animal, as they had never heard of a goatafrow before. She told them it lived only on steep hill sides, or it would starve other-wise, since its uphill side had short legs, and the down hill side had long legs. Thus the goatafrow made his way around the mountain sides, feeding on the sparse bunch grass. The eastern people were on the alert to catch a glimpse of them on the steep mountain sides, and no doubt felt disappointed when none were seen.

An Unusual Childhood

Our Dad told us they had come upon a lake, apparently not known of before. He and Uncle Dave named it "Charlie White" lake, I suppose after someone they both knew. It was quite big and green-deep. It was surrounded by a bowl-like chain of mountains, with rugged rimrock almost all the way around. There were cave like holes in the rock rims, and at night a cougar startled everyone with his hair-raising scream. No doubt the caves made perfect dens.

The fishing was unbelievable, they were large and hungry. We were promised that we would get to go to Charlie White Lake, when we were older. The cougars shared their surroundings with huge, hungry mosquitoes, but that wasn't considered a problem.

Some of the mountains near home had rocky rims and shallow caves, which we explored. The caves were home to a lot of pack rats, with their messy stick-built nests. Also, many a badger lived in holes in these rocks, they would come out and sit up, paws crossed over their chests, and whistle at us.

The folks caught a lot of them, thinking their fur should be valuable; Mom had a trunk-full of their soft grey-brown fur, only to find there was no market for them. We explored a lot of these caves, and considered living in them. We talked of letting our hair grow long and bushy, and wearing badger-skin clothes. We imagined ourselves living on wild berries, greens and whatever we could find that was edible.

The sunny summer days were perfect for such plans, but as fall approached, the idea was gone. The beautiful Indian summer came, the trees became fantastic and we hated the thought of going back to school. Mom was sewing again, and all our potatoes, rutabagas and onions were stored in the hillside cellar. It had double doors, one outer door, then a space, and the inner door. The vegetables kept well, in no danger of freezing. We started riding to school; we took a short cut across Casey's place and down a steep hill to the road to Jardine.

The days were long, as we got up while it was still dark. We had to catch our horses that had been turned out in the hay field. Then after fighting over who got which saddle, we had our horses ready, and ate a big dish of oatmeal and if we had time, put away a pile of sour dough hotcakes. The horses were always frisky, except Rock, and we would make a good start.

We lost time going uphill to Casey's and sometimes Mrs. Casey would come out with cookies for us. It didn't pay to hurry by, in case she might not see us. Then after leaving Casey house, we had a long flat stretch, where we got our horses going as fast as they could.

Even Paint would run, though he was small and handi-capped, only Rock would start running, and then quit. Clyde had a bad time with Rock. He would whip and kick Rock, but Rock just put a little faster walk. He was always way behind. I can still picture Clyde beating his steed and yelling, "Wait for me," on this trek. We passed "Little Round Tap", a small hill perfectly round and pointed at the top, like a volcano. It was covered with lava rock and the Mon-tana state flower, Bitterroot, grew there.

Next came a pond, screened by willows, it nearly always had wild ducks, even after a thin sheet of ice froze on it. We tried to ap-proach quietly, but the ducks always flew away as we went by. The worst part of this route to school was next, a steep mountain that went down almost to the Jardine road. I know our horses hated this part as much as we did, the trail was zigzagged in an effort to lessen the steepness, but even then, the saddles would work up on the horses' necks, and we would have to stop, and push the saddles back in place, cinch up, and start on our way.

At the bottom of the mountains there was a small stream, where the horses insisted on getting a drink. Then it was across a small hillside and down the bank, onto the Jardine road, where we whipped the horses into a run. We always took them to our small barn, where Daddy had left hay. Then we ran for school, nearly al-ways late. Our teacher told us off, but she finally became accustomed to our late arrival.

It didn't seem to make much difference in our grades. After school it was the same trip in reverse, the horses lunged up the steep-est places, then their saddles slid back on them. If any of us rode double, as sometimes did happen, the rider behind the saddle had to hold on tight or slide over the back end of the horses.

Once Clyde was riding on Dot with me, I in the saddle (I was the owner, therefore the boss). We were quarreling about something, so Clyde was mad at me. He wouldn't hold on to me so he slid over Dot's rear end and she kicked him when he hit the ground. Clyde didn't like horses.

When we got home we had to take care of the horses first, then hobble them and turn them loose. When hobbled, they could eat all they wanted, but couldn't outrun us in the morning. This made long days and no one had to coax us to eat and get to bed.

As the fall turned to winter, it seemed we were getting later and later, although it would be dark when we went after our horses. Our hands and feet would warm up and tingle. It finally got impossible to get to school on time, especially after the snow began.

Our teacher once quoted, "A dollar, a dollar, a 10' O clock scholar, why do you come so soon, you used to come at 10' O clock, but now you come at noon." There was nothing we could do about, it so we had to move back to the Jardine house.

Daddy made his fall trip to Gardiner, and got our winter groceries: flour by the 100-pound sack, sugar, coffee, and, what was a real treat, a box of Big-Y apples from Washington state. We were allowed a half apple each evening. They were so good, each apple wrapped in purple paper. The whole box was eaten up before they had time to spoil. The only other apples we had were early summer apples, grown on the Blanding ranch, near Gardiner. We usually got some of them every summer, Mom made apple butter and some jelly with them.

So here we were in Jardine again, with not much to do beside school work. We snooped around a lot. There was a big tank, a discard of the mining company that we were curious about. It lay on its side in a vacant lot. There was a hole in one end that we could squeeze through, so we did. It was rusty inside and out, it was almost more then we could stand, to be in the tank, and have someone

58

Harlene Jessie Reeves

pound on the outside with a stick.

Once we were up Bear Creek, we explored in the trees near the road and found a moonshine still. We didn't know what it was, but asked Daddy and he told us to stay away as it was dangerous if the owner found out we had seen it.

The winter went as usual, except for Christmas. After the school held their program, the men threw money on the floor, pennies, nickels, dimes and some quarters. It was a wild scramble to pick up the money, but everyone got some of it.

On Christmas Eve, we were in bed, and we heard Santa Claus go by, the bells on his team tinkling off toward J. Rose's house. The next day we looked for reindeer track in the snow, but all we found were dog tracks, going to Jack Rose's house. We asked him if he had heard the bells, he said he had and they seemed to have crossed Bear Creek and gone over the mountains past the mill. There were no tracks on the snow-covered ice of Bear Creek. That was the nearest we got to Santa Claus. But we did get hard candy, nuts and apples and some new clothes.

Fanny had some puppies that were about a year old. We kept one of them and some of the people in town took the others. Daddy kept Fanny at the ranch. Sometimes Daddy came after us on weekends and brought milk for us in Jardine.

Then an old man, old Sullivan, came to our place. He was a civil war veteran. He told us how he fought the battle of Shiloh. He had long white hair and beard. At first we loved to listen to his bloody tales of the battle of Shiloh. Then we got tired of him.

He wanted a place to stay, so my Dad took him to the ranch to help with the chores, even though he was old, he was pretty spry. Old Sullivan claimed to be an inventor also. Once we got him we couldn't figure out how to get rid of him. He was nearly ninety years old, but didn't want to go to a veteran's home.

Winter went on forever, we were tired of the snow, except for the times it froze on top, and we could walk anywhere. We could even cross Bear Creek, and in the holes in the ice we could lie down and see the icy water rushing under us.

Then a great thing happened, the arsenic eater got married! They moved into a little house across the road from ours. One night right after Mr. and Mrs. Arsenic eater moved in, there was a terrible clamor at their house, cans jangling, someone pounding on a wash tub, horns blowing and people yelling. We were afraid at first, but the folks were laughing, they said it was a Chivaree, and always happened to newlyweds.

Their house was dark, but they soon lit their lamps and the noise stopped, and all the people went in. We asked if we could go and to our surprise, we were allowed. We went in, the door was open, and everyone was laughing and talking, no one seemed to notice us.

There was lots of candy for everyone, the grown-ups didn't seem to eat much but we did. I don't remember our folks going; my Dad had a strange pride of not owing anything to anyone, or of taking anything for free. We were not bothered that way; we stayed at the Arsenic eater's house till way late.

We were sitting on a blanket covered trunk and could hardly keep our eyes open, but didn't want to leave as long as there was still candy. Finally our folks came after us. Everyone was having such a good time I don't think they knew we had gone. That's when I decided to be a bachelor.

We were so weary of snow that we decided to climb a hill north of Jardine, where the big spruce trees were growing here and there. It was real hard going as we wallowed, up to our waists in snow, until we reached the trees. Under each tree there was bare ground where the trees protected the sparse, dry grass and cones. We made our slow way from tree to tree, toward the hill top. We had a fine view, looking down on Jardine, and in the clear, cold air the steady thump-thump of the stamping mill was quite plain.

We didn't want to go back, so we made our lunging crawl to the top of the hill. Here it was flat and wind-blown, the snow in deeper drifts. It was frozen, so we could walk on top of the snow easily. Not so lucky was a thin cow elk, she was up to her neck in snow, and by the torn snow about her, we could see she had been trying to fight her way out. She was so tired that she saw us and made desperate attempts to move, but was too feeble.

She watched us. We walked up to her, but didn't dare touch her, as she shook her head and snorted. We were so sorry for her plight, we spent the rest of the day, going back to the big trees, where we pulled all the dry grass we could find and fought our way back to the elk. She snorted and tried to lunge away, but finally started eating the tiny pile of dead grass. We reluctantly left her to go home, and when we went over the hill, the last glimpse we saw, she had her head up, watching us and eating her grass. The next day, it snowed some more so we couldn't go back, and as day after day passed, with new snow storms, we never got back.

Spring finally came, with its ponds and rivulets of water. We became brave and went up to the cemetery—graveyard, as it was called. The graveyard was up past the mills, and dated way back. Mom said it was old when she was a girl. She didn't like us to go there, as she had been a pall-bearer for a small baby, whose parents had asked for four young girls, dressed in white, to carry their baby to its grave. It must have been a sad thing for the four children; anyway, Mom never forgot her experience.

We liked the graveyard; it had huge, beautiful markers, with such sad epitaphs. The grass was tall and matted, as no one ever cut it. We always expected a scary experience, but usually it was quiet and sunny when we were there. At one time, we were trying to read a small marker in the tall grass, and all at once the grass went flat in a perfect rectangle, leaving the grass around it straight and tall. We all left as fast as we could.

After we got safely out the gate, we stopped to consider the matter. So all together, we crept back to investigate. The little rectangle of grass was still flattened. On close investigation, we discovered that this small grave had been covered by a folding wire frame, no doubt for a covering of flowers. It had rusted and grass grown

61

through it, and when one of us touched the corner, it just collapsed.

Many of the markers had doves, lambs and angels on them. One of them was of polished granite, square at the bottom and tapering gracefully to the top. On it we read, "Farewell, Dear Mother, Sweet Thy Rest." It was my favorite gravestone. The cemetery is still there, one of the newest graves near the gate says, "WELCOME", it is the grave of George Welcome. He went to school with my mother. It has won the distinction of being the only cemetery in the United States with Welcome at the gate.

Our cows got out, since it was spring, and they wandered way off to Buffalo Flats. Mom and I and one of the boys went after them, it was long after dark, and seemed the longest walk I ever made. We didn't happen to have a horse so it was a tiring trip, but I sort of enjoyed it, I hadn't been to Buffalo Flats since before I was born.

In the dark, it wasn't anything special, but we did go by Mrs. Morrison's Fox Farm. She had a big house, and a lady to live with her, and a man to do the work. Some of the kids around town said she had glass door knobs on all the doors, which seemed incredible.

Quite a few families left Jardine, as the mining slowed down. We went through their vacant houses, even though they were boarded up and locked. We never found anything good; all that was left were old newspapers or old clothes. Even most of the furniture was gone. We did catch a big Persian cat, but it didn't stay with us.

Finally school was out again and back to the ranch, the best place in the world, we thought. Old Sullivan was still there. He insisted that he should live in our hillside cellar. He didn't want us to bother him. Our Dad put a small cook stove and stove pipe up through the roof so the old man could cook for himself. Old Sullivan called it a dugout and seemed to be fighting the battle of Shiloh over again. He kept on the alert for rebels and made us a little uneasy, as we weren't sure what a rebel was and how to act if one did show up.

Mom was upset because old Sullivan stayed in the cellar, and didn't come to eat. We would climb up by the chimney and try to find out what he was doing. Whenever we caught him out of the cellar, he would say he was inventing.

The only invention we ever saw was a pie-shaped piece of concrete and cow or dog hair mix. It was dry and hard, and good for nothing. Still, the old man stayed on, in the cellar. He would come out once in awhile, to get wood for his stove, and that was about the only time we saw him. He was a problem.

As usual we wandered all over the horse pasture, cow pasture and the range land. There was a huge rock, it stuck out of the hill-side, it was as big as a room. We couldn't get up on it and were a little afraid as it was cube-shaped and only one corner was buried in the earth, and a steep hillside below. We did get on the uphill side and push, trying to roll it down the hill.

We also wandered up past Teddy's Hill and took a trail that came out at Parkers. We went to Perry's grave, with its four trees, and stood around, remembering. Somehow, we weren't afraid of this grave, like the ones in Jardine. Perry never had a marker on his grave. Parker's never knew we were there; we were so close to their house, we could hear them.

During the summer, we went to Blandings to get apples. They were white colored apples, and not as good as the big, red apples of winter. But they made good pies, jelly and apple butter. We could scramble up the trees and reach the apples that Mom couldn't reach.

Bud climbed a tree and there was a big snake in it. It opened its mouth and hissed at Bud and Bud reached over and put his finger in its mouth. Mom was really scared, she was sure it was a poisonous snake, and we cried just a little bit, as we were sure Bud would die.

We went to the Blandings house, and Mom told her what had happened. Mrs. Blanding wasn't a bit sympathetic. She said it was a harmless blacksnake and there were a lot of them around. We went home with the apples, and Bud was perfectly all right.

Many times, when we had to go after the horses or cows we scared up grouse. They hated to fly very far, so would just get up on a tree branch and sit there like they were paralyzed. We could throw rocks at them and they would just sit tight. Finally we would hit one in the right place, and carry it home for supper. They were far better to eat than chicken.

Then there were porcupine. They were easy to hit and kill, the problem was the skinning, but their meat was white and tasted very much like pork.

Off in the timber up Eagle Creek, we often heard Partridge drumming--they sounded a lot like a Model T car starting up. A few people were getting cars. There were Stars, Hupmobiles, Velie, and of course Model T's - lots of them. We still had our horses and buggies, and my Dad got a surrey with the fringe on top. It was fancy, with red leather upholstery. It was stored in the shed with my Dad's old pool table. He had part-ownership in a saloon in Gardiner, with his half-brother, Burley Douthett. This was before he was married. The saloon had been sold, Daddy got married and Burley went back to Kentucky.

Along in June, one day, Mom took Sylvia, Burl and Bud with her to Gardiner. Clyde and I were left to look after things. It was a warm day, and a long day. We were hungry, but didn't want to cook. Clyde wished we had some ice cream. We had a hand operated freezer and lots of milk and cream. We mixed up the sugar, milk and cream, and some vanilla, like we had seen Mom do. Our problem was--no ice. We took off up Eagle Creek, above the house, and followed it to where it went underground.

There where it disappeared among some roots, was ice. By digging back along the creek's course, we uncovered lots of ice. It had dirt and moss in it but that didn't matter. We hurried home with our ice; it took both of us to carry it. We packed it in our freezer and broke up some of the cows' salt block. Then we took turns cranking it. It seemed to take forever, but was finally ready to eat. So Clyde and I were sitting and eating big amounts of good ice cream, when Mom and the others came home. Of course we had to share, Mom didn't say much, probably too surprised.

We took turns, during the summer, riding to Jardine for the

mail. Once I went, riding Dot. She had just gone by Casey's Lake, when she suddenly shied off to the right, and started running. No matter how I tried to stop or turn her, she seemed to be going faster, she left the trail and went plunging through the tall sage brush, jumping the higher ones, and went at a full gallop, away from the trail.

There was a hill with a small stream at the bottom, she galloped full speed down the hill, and jumped across the stream. I had all I could do, just to stay on. We traveled full speed up the next hill and then Dot stopped at the top. She turned and looked back, her ears up and snorting. I looked too, but couldn't see anything. I told my parents about it, since we had to go the long way around to Jardine. Dot refused to go back to the short-cut trail. Mom and Daddy decided that there was a bear, which I didn't get a chance to see, but Dot either smelled or saw it.

We did a lot of exploring since we could ride. Once we went up Bear Creek and out on top of the hill where we had fed the cow elk. It was depressing though, because we found her skeleton. She hadn't gone too far.

Jardine was a horrible town in the summer, hot and with crickets singing everywhere. Many of the homes were empty, we found some starving kittens, it took several hours to catch them, and they were wild. We put them in a sack and they rode home with us. We fed them all they could eat, so with big bellies, they laid down and died. Mom said they had been empty so long, the food killed them.

Fanny's puppy, the one we kept, disappeared; we found him a long time later. He had been dead a long time. He probably had found and eaten one of the poisoned gophers.

One of the worst things was when I got in a fight with Clyde, he was chasing me, and as I ran ahead, I spied a dead, swollen rabbit. No doubt, it had eaten poisoned oats. As I ran, I jumped over the dead animal, and almost without thinking, picked the swollen carcass up, turned and threw it at Clyde. He hadn't time to turn away. It hit him right across the face, and, Erp! It burst. Poor Clyde, it made him

An Unusual Childhood

sick. I was ashamed and sorry; I didn't know the awful thing would pop open like that.

On windy days, we often climbed one of the leafy trees, as near to the top as we dared. There we could wrap our arms and legs about the tree and the wind would sway us back and forth, just like the Rock-a-bye Baby.

Another thing we enjoyed was playing in our Dad's black-smith shop. He made his own horseshoes, so he had a fairly well-equipped shop. There was the grindstone, the glowing coals that could be coaxed into white heat by pumping air on them with the bellows. We spent a lot of time there, heating nails to white hot, and dropping them in a pail of water. They made a great sizzle and steam. Then we would fish them out with our pliers, as they were still hot, heat them over again, and drop them in the water again.

One day, I think we were all there, except Sylv, it was crowd-ed in the shop, with all of us jumping the bellows, heating our nails and sizzling them. I had taken a white-hot nail, turned around with it, to drop it in the water, and Burl was standing there. My nail went right through his cheek, making a perfect, square hole. He said it didn't hurt much; he could blow air in and out of it. It healed, but he has a dimple-like scar on his cheek yet.

One summer, our relations from Michigan came to visit. They were awed at the mountains, and the view we had, looking down and far away was Mammoth, and the Hot Springs in Yellow-stone Park.

Just above our house there was a clearing, surrounded by gi-ant spruce trees. It was a beautiful spot, except for one thing, Daddy had built our new out-house in the very center of the little meadow. We never thought much of it, until these eastern relatives laughed about it. Grandma Cutler was with these people, she was really our great-grand mother.

They had a cousin with them, she was about 18, and had beautiful red hair. It was put up and coiled around her head. When she brushed it in the mornings, we were startled to see her hair almost to her ankles. It had never been cut.

Great Grandma Cutler had brought shoes for each of us. I had always wanted the kind she gave me, they were Black Patent, long, almost to the knees, with buckled straps, almost like high-top sandals. I was very sad to find they were too small, and hurt my feet.

Grandma said she would get a bigger pair, but I didn't want to wait another ten years or so, so I bawled, begged and made myself a disgusting sight. I hunted for the shoes, so Grandma said it was too late, as she had thrown them in the creek, just below the bridge where it was deep.

It was a good way to get rid of me, as I spent most of the time after that wading the creek, looking for the shoes. I never did find them. After all our company left, we resumed our normal lives.

Mom had the farm work to do, with whatever help she could get out of us. We had to go through the potato field, picking off the big potato bugs. There were never many of them so we got them before they killed the vines.

There were always the cows to bring home, and we got the job of riding the fence in the horse pasture. One night we found the cows, but Holliday was missing. We remembered how she had surprised us before, but she didn't come back the next day. The second day, she was still missing, so Mom got her horse and searched all the range area, where the cows usually went, still no Holliday.

We were sure she was dead, but for several more days, we looked for her. We went through the thick brush and wild berry patches, and in the tall stinky weeds. Mom even sent the boys to Parkers to see if they had seen her. No, was all we heard.

It was time to clean the hillside cellar, to get all the left-over sprouted vegetables out. Old Sullivan had moved out. He had gone way up Eagle Creek and built a shack of boughs, where he talked to himself and amazed himself over the Battle of Shiloh.

We were not worried about him, since Mom had smelled

burning feathers, and caught the old man spreading corn at the outside cellar door, and when the chickens gathered to eat the corn, the wily old man would grab one. He was cleaning them in the cellar and burning the feathers--he had a steady diet of chicken and our stored vegetables. We were to take his stove out and rake all the old vegetables out.

We opened the first door. The second didn't open very well, we got it partially open and there was Holliday! She was so full of vegetables and sprouts, her stomach bulged. We finally got her to back up, as she was trying to push the door open, and it closed tighter. She was just a dumb cow, and didn't realize she was closing herself in. She bulged so fat, she could hardly get out the door and when she finally squeezed through, she ran for water. She had lived all those days on vegetables and sprouts.

We went again to where our ditch was being dug. Mom helped shoveling dirt away while Daddy cut roots and cleared away logs. Clyde and I got in a fight, Clyde clobbered me over the head and I thought I was dying, the blood running over my face. No doubt he was getting even for the dead rabbit episode.

We had a lunch of cold liver sandwiches and milk--it was the best sandwich I ever ate. After we started to go home, my Dad called Sylv to help him. He gave her a shovel and said to start digging; he had found the skeleton of the old Austrian.

The poor man had died during the winter. Someone had found him and reported it to one of the rangers. A ranger, or rangers, had gone to investigate, and since there was deep snow, and the ground was frozen, they had simply buried him in the snow. The always hungry coyotes had done the rest. It was hard on Sylv to help gather the scattered bones and bury them.

Somewhere in Europe, the woman and her children waited in vain.

After the burial, Mom and we kids went back home. We were big enough now to help get the hay in, Mom driving the team and pitching the hay for our bare feet to trample down. It seemed like every year our hay fields were bigger and the stacks longer. We had tunnels under them, even when it was cold it was warm in the haystacks. We set some traps and caught some gophers. We made a wire pen for them, where they lived a miserable life, and gave us fleas. They finally died, and had a fine funeral.

About this time Mom got a new washing machine. It saved a lot of labor for Mom, all she had to do was carry the water from the creek, heat it in a huge tub over a fire, when it was hot, it was carried to the machine. The clothes and home-made soap were put in, and we got to pull the lever back and forth. This made the soap, water and clothes go back and forth in the machine till they were clean. We had to take turns on the lever, as it made our arms ache. Sometimes the boys disappeared on wash day.

One of the worst things happened to Dot. She had a filly colt. It was cute, but a Dad-burned pest. It had to go wherever Dot went and seemed to choose some of the most embarrassing times to want to eat. It would run alongside Dot when I was riding and then dart in front so Dot would have to stop. It was a pretty filly, bright bay with white blazed face, and four white stockings. She was a pest but so cute we put up with her.

This summer we got a letter from Mom's youngest sister, Babe. She and her husband Raymond, and children, Patty, Irene and "Little Man," whose real name was Raymond. Uncle Raymond was a motorcycle cop in San Diego. He had been asked to resign, because he had been trying to stop a running criminal, and in shooting at the man's legs he had missed and killed the man. He had a motorcycle with a sidecar. Babe and the three children rode in the sidecar from San Diego to our place. I don't know how they stood it.

We got the letter, and everyday after that we went up the lane over and over to see if they were coming. It was a long time before they actually arrived, tired and happy. We had been so anxious to see them, but when they finally arrived, we disappeared to a safe place where we could stare at our cousins.

Little Man didn't matter; it was the little girls who we stared at. They had short hair with bangs, and dresses so short we could see their matching pants. They also wore short socks and slippers. We were dressed in anything available, bib overalls, old school clothes and barefoot. We gradually came out of hiding. The cousins were not at all shy, and we were friends.

At supper that first night, Aunt asked the blessing, we were embarrassed, as we had never encountered such a thing before. She said they were Seventh-Day-Adventists, which made no sense to us. When bedtime came, Patty and Irene were to sleep with Sylv and me. We went to bed, and to our surprise, Patty and Irene knelt at the bed and said prayers. We argued with them after we were all in bed. Patty didn't say much, but Irene said she would tell on us the next night.

We had a good time the next day, we showed Patty and Irene all our best playing places, and some of them, like the old playhouse, their mother had played there. The main trouble was Aunt's before-meal prayer; she got tired of it herself and made other people do it. Next she made us take a bath every night, and while we were in the tub, she would bring a bucket of cold water and pour it over our heads.

Then Irene started telling on us if we didn't say our bedtime prayers. Aunt would come up with a switch and make us do it. We got so we didn't like Irene at all. Her mother had her do little enter-tainments in the evenings. She would sing and dance the Charleston, which we thought a silly thing to do. Patty didn't act that way at all. Patty would sneak breakfast bacon under her plate and eat it later, where her sharp-eyed sister wasn't watching.

One evening when Irene was doing the Charleston for her proud parents and her silent Aunt and Uncle, her mother remarked, "My, isn't she light on her feet!" We had to leave in a hurry, it sound-ed so funny, and Daddy had winked at us.

That night, when we went to bed, we refused to say our prayers, so Irene ran downstairs, and told her mother. Here came Aunt with her switch, and we really got a working over, after which we three knelt at the bedside and mumbled a prayer, with Aunt standing over with her switch. She made our brothers pray, too. Mom didn't say anything, but went outdoors for awhile. We wanted her to take our part, but she said Aunt was company and we had to be nice to her.

We all went up to the horse corral one day; we drank the good, cold water and made fun of Irene. She was already mad because we had run all the way, and wouldn't wait for her. We were licking the salt block and Irene said she was going to tell on us, as we were not supposed to eat salt.

We got mad and broke off a bunch of willows and started switching at Irene and telling her to dance. Patty didn't hit her sister at first, but when Irene started screaming and running for home, we all chased her, switching her legs and calling her tattle-tale. We chased her all the way to the house, and we sure got a whipping. Irene had welts on her legs, her Mom was really angry.

After we had our punishment, we went to the barn and had hysterics. Later, we coaxed Irene onto Paint, telling her how gentle he was, he was bareback, and had no bridle. It would have been all right, but we walked behind Paint and hit him with everything we could pick up. Irene hung on, but was screaming, and the more she screamed, the faster Paint ran for the barn. Irene came loose about halfway, and Aunt ran to her rescue. She wasn't hurt, but her feelings were. Aunt was livid with anger and they decided to leave.

We rode the side-car to the gate where our fence line ran. We stayed awhile and hunted for the scissors I had thrown away when our house was burning. We never did find them, but we were rid of Irene - so light on her feet.

Finally came the time when we packed up, took a lot of camp gear and pack horses and went to Charlie White Lake. It seemed to take forever. We had never gone so far from home before. We had stopped in Jardine and got our mail on the way. We had been reading the funny papers, especially Mutt and Jeff and the adventures of the little boy, Mutt's nephew.

He had been lost and had found a cave, underground--there was a city of gold. It was scary. We read it over and over, and wondered what awful fate lay ahead for the little boy. When we finally arrived at the lake, we were too tired to be hungry.

Mom and Daddy were anxious to start fishing as the fish were jumping all over. It was almost dark, so the folks told us they would fish for a short time and come back to cook something. The horses and pack animals were unloaded, and were tied up.

The mosquitoes hadn't had a good meal for a long time, so we fixed up our beds, taking the horse blankets as more covers, it seemed to suddenly get cold. We went to sleep, heads under covers. The smell of the horse blankets was almost too much, but we kept them on.

I remember dreaming we were with the little boy, lost in the golden city, when a cougar let out a dying woman-like scream. We were glad when our parents came back, in the dark. They had caught enough fish to have for supper. The next day wasn't so bad, but I had no faith in that lake, where our parents had to wade out through reeds to reach deep water. I expected anything, the bottom going out from under them in the reeds, or cougars creeping out of their caves.

The horses shared my doubts. We were glad to move on; we had a lot of fish to take home, packed in wet reed grass, where they kept fresh. On our way back, we stopped at Fish Lake. Here, the fish were waiting for us. The camp we had at Fish Lake was much nicer. The land sloped down to the water.

On the other side of the lake was a big mountain, that looked as if it had been cut in half, the lake was right up to the cut side, there was no other half. Perhaps in volcanic times, it had slid down into the lake. For about three feet at the water's edge, it was clear and shallow, then it was blue-green deep, it must have been very deep.

The fishing was good, and we stayed for two days. We had so many fish, even after a steady diet, that we had to go home where we could share with the Jones family, who had volunteered to look after things. Clyde had a bad time; he was sick of fish and sick of riding.

On the way home, Bud and Clyde rode Paint double. We all had new cowboy hats; five white hats in a row. I guess we looked pretty funny to my Dad. There was snow here and there, we rode around it. At one place the going was narrow, between a small lake and a big snow drift.

There was a tree in our way, but by ducking our heads we rode under its big branch. We were going single file, Clyde and Bud behind when one of them yelled. We all stopped and Daddy was laughing—somehow, when Paint went under the low limb, one of the boys had ducked his head and the other ended up astride the horse, facing its tail, but hadn't even lost his hat. We had no more incidents on the homeward journey.

Mrs. Jones was happy to see all the fish, she cooked a big fish dinner, and we had to eat more fish. We were satisfied to be home and drop in the same old routines. My father went to work for Blandings, the apple tree people, they needed help clearing land and hauling their hay into their barn. It was a huge barn, with the hay stored in the upper story.

Mr. Blanding was getting old and not too well, but Mrs. Blanding was a hard-hearted case to work for. There were several men working there, they had their meals and sleeping bunks, besides the stingy wage, as Mrs. Blanding was a tight-wad. Daddy came home on week-ends, to help get our work done, and to get a change of diet, as Mrs. Blanding had gotten into a rut, and fed the crew corned beef and sour-dough biscuits meal after meal.

Mr. Blanding was known as Old Jim. He did some of the lighter chores and was close by when the hay was being put in the barn. One day when the crew was washing up on the outside bench (cold water, soap and towels furnished), Mrs. Blanding went to the barn to check up on her husband. There was a terrible shriek, "There goes Jim, down the chute!"

It seems the old man had climbed up in the loft to spread the hay about, he didn't see or made a misstep, and down the chute into the manger went Old Jim. There was hay in the manger, so Jim was unhurt, although the Mrs. gave him a good working over with her tongue. My Dad wanted to leave the job, as Mrs. Blanding was a regular battle-axe, but stayed for Old Jim's sake.

An Unusual Childhood

One day after a tasty meal of biscuits and Corned Beef, Old Jim drew my Dad to one side; out of sight of Mrs. Blanding. He said, "Harley, I like you and want you too see something." He took my Dad down into their cellar-like basement, where it was dark and cool. There was a barrel in the corner with a lid over it.

Old Jim took the lid off and said, "Look for yourself. This is where the Mrs. keeps the corned beef." Old Jim lit a lantern and lowered it part way into the barrel. Daddy looked and about gagged. There was about half a barrel of corned beef that seemed to be moving about somehow. There was something wrong with it—it looked white in places. On closer inspection, my Dad saw the meat was working with maggots. He had to leave, and came home to stay until he could find another job. He could always work on the ditch. It was getting nearer Parker's, and we wondered it Parkers would let the ditch be dug across their land.

We didn't see much of the Parkers. Once, Geraldine stopped by to show us her new horse. It was a pretty, small horse, almost yellow in color. She told us she never put her feet on the ground, as she kept a horse at their house all the time, even when she went to their barn--not very far; she rode. She called her new horse, Yellow Hammer, which was the name of a bird or woodpecker type.

She told us that Ruth Ellen had been sick a long time, then gouged her spurs into poor Yellow Hammer, and took off at a gallop. Poor, pretty Yellow Hammer, he was soon a wretched, worn-out crow bait of a horse, and Geraldine had a new one to replace him. Mom started thinking about Ruth Ellen, daughter of an old friend, and decided to go see if she could help. I and Sylv went, too.

We were eager to see our former friends. When we got there, Amy seemed to be the only one home. Mrs. Parker's house was a mess. Amy said Ruth Ellen was upstairs. Amy didn't go up with us, and the little twin, Jiggs hid somewhere.

We went up to Ruth Ellen's room, where she lay in a dirty bed, her chamber pot, full to over-flowing, stunk up the whole room. She had been vomiting, too and no one had cleaned up after her. She was glad to see us, and cried. We could hardly believe that Ruth Ellen could look so bad. Her long hair was tangled and matted in back and she was so thin she seemed a different girl.

Mom got mad, she said she was going to stay until Jim came home. She got some water heated, and told us to go outside. We didn't go back, but Mom said she tried to do some cleaning up and emptied the pot. We waited till way late. Geraldine came home. She said her Dad didn't come home on some nights. We went on home, later we heard that Ruth Ellen was in the hospital in Livingston, she had appendicitis.

One day Mom had to go to Gardiner and we all went with her in the pretty new surrey. Pat and Rock were the lucky horses that took us. Rock had a bad habit of going to sleep while walking. We came to Z Hill, it was a steep hill, winding down to Gardiner.

On one of the curves there was a drop-off right at the road curve. Rock had gone to sleep, and in spite of Mom yelling at him to stop, he kept going straight ahead. Mom leaped to the road and ran up and grabbed Rock's bridle and stopped him before he stepped off the edge. Poor old Pat was trying to hold back.

We went to Hall's store in Gardiner, where we could buy just about anything. Not only that, but we could eat all the crackers we wanted, free, and one of the Halls sometimes gave us striped candy.

Aunt Sadie and Uncle Dave had moved to Gardiner. They lived in a small, white house right on the brink of Yellowstone River. There were huge rocks in Aunt's yard and along the trail to the out-house. The outhouse was below the house and sat in solitary splendor above the river.

Aunt had planted flowers among the rocks, it was very pretty. There were yellow poppies among the rocks on the way to the out-house, it seemed like a fairyland to us. The outhouse itself was not the usual thing. Aunt had put pink striped wallpaper on the walls and a braided rug on the floor. There were vases of flowers sitting here and there. The flowers were made of bright-colored paper.

We would have loved to use the outhouse for a play house.

An Unusual Childhood

There was even a Sears Roebuck catalogue handy. Aunt told us that it wasn't a good place to play; for one thing, it was perched in a precarious place above the river below.

Aunt also did some painting. She had a huge painting of a frightened elk leaping a log, with a forest fire among the trees behind him. This painting was made so it could be used as a screen. Aunt would put a light behind the painting and it seemed like a real fire. We always had a cake when we visited Aunt Sadie. Mom could leave us there and go about her business, and Aunt always was glad we came.

She also had a stereoscope, with lots of pictures to look at. Near their house was a path to a swinging bridge over the river. It was a long way across, and the river was way below. It was supported by cables on each side, we often had to cross on it, and it would start swinging as we neared the center. We learned to look at the opposite side to keep from getting dizzy. Once we forgot and looked down, it became so scary, we felt like crawling the whole length of the bridge. Now this bridge has been replaced by a modern concrete structure.

The Jones family had moved to Gardiner, too, as some of Jardine's mines had closed when they ran out of a paying lode. We sometimes visited them, and also some people who had twin girls, Lela and Lyla. Another lady Mom liked had dirty kids and blue willow dishes. I admired the dishes and wished we had them. Once we were in Gardiner, and Mom took the lady with the dirty kids with us.

We went on the road to Mammoth, to where some Chinese grew a vegetable garden. They sold vegetables to passing tourists. We stopped there for awhile, but one of the Chinese took one of our hats off and put it on himself. He had a long pig-tail, and said he was going to keep the hat, we were afraid of such strange looking people, and some of the kids were crying, so we went back to Gardiner.

Our Dad had gone to work and we were left with the work at home. The summers were short at our elevation, (7000 feet), but we had a long, beautiful Indian Summer. We had planted more potatoes and they had to be dug and picked up by hand. Any that were left were frozen. When they were all in, Mom was sick; there was just too much work for her. It was nearing school time again, and we were considered old enough to go to the Jardine house and take care of ourselves, as Daddy needed help.

We had more horses and cattle than ever. The haystacks were long and surrounded by a high fence to keep elk out. Daddy had to keep adding more fence, making it higher, as the snow got deeper and packed.

Once, Mom went through the wire fence and climbed up to where the hay was being cut and thrown down, and met a big bull elk. He had jumped the fence, and climbed up on the hay, eaten his fill and lay down to sleep. Mom said she had never slid down the hay and left so fast. She ran all the way, slipping and falling in the snow. She got the rifle and went back to the hay stack, but the elk had gone.

We were old enough to look out for ourselves, now. We were riding to school, again. When the snow got too deep, we moved to the house in Jardine. Our folks supplied flour, sugar, potatoes and other groceries. We didn't keep a cow then, so Mom came to Jardine and brought milk. I remember once, on coming home from school, the jar of milk was left on the porch, and it had frozen so hard it stuck up completely out of its container.

We would come home from school, cut wood, and start a fire in the range, the house was cold and seemed to heat slowly. We cooked potatoes and made awful biscuits. We could have made good stews, but were usually too hungry to wait, so ate our spuds and biscuits. We often went without breakfasts and hurried to school, where it was warm.

Once an old man, German by birth, came to our house while we were in school, he cut and stacked a lot of wood and had a fire going in the stove. It was a real luxury to come home to a warm home. Evidently he didn't approve of our way of life, as several times we came home to find a stew cooked and hot rolls and jelly. We didn't know who did this for us, but we were embarrassed and almost indignant.

Sylvia made friends with Johnny K's mother. She invited

An Unusual Childhood

Sylv to stop at her place and have lunch with them, which Sylv was happy to do. Sylv wasn't afraid of Johnny, and he looked forward to seeing her go by to school. He never learned to say Sylvia, but called her "Elsie." He would stand on the porch and when Sylv went by, he would pound the rail and call, "Elsie!"

His Mom told Sylv that he had been a normal, extra-smart boy, but had fallen off the roof and had been insane ever since. We wouldn't go near him for all the tea and eggs in the town. That was their main diet. Sylv ate with them quite often, leaving me and the boys to cook for ourselves. She was the best cook, so we didn't eat so well when she didn't come home.

Once we burned some trash, and put whole potatoes in the fire to bake. Unfortunately there was some old rubber in the trash, which gave our potatoes an undesirable taste.

On weekends, Mom would come for us. We sure appreciated the stews and pies of fried apples and apricots with canned milk, as the cows were dry. Once we got home just as Daddy had put a huge roast out to cool in the snow. It was a badger, which he had skinned and cleaned and cooked for the dogs. It was still hot, and crusty-brown, when we arrived. We started picking off tasty pieces and eating it, until Daddy came by and stopped us.

That badger sure tasted good in spite of the fact he had a foot missing, probably from being in a trap at some time. After the weekend was over, Mom took us back to Jardine, with a supply of vegetables, and lots of advice.

We found more old carbide lamps, which we took apart to remove the carbide. It was fascinating stuff. One evening, Clyde made some cookies. He forgot about the carbide on the table. It looked a lot like the flour, so he accidentally got some of it mixed with the dough when he rolled out the cookies. His batch of cookies didn't turn out so well, so we didn't eat them. Since they were Clyde's cookies, he sampled them. He got pretty sick, and we got scared.

Our first thought was to go home to the ranch, in spite of the snow. We left, down the road toward Gardiner, but when we got

Harlene Jessie Reeves

to the short-cut we were so scared we decided to climb the steep hill. The trail was buried under the snow, which we plowed through, forcing Clyde along. He was so miserable he kept lying down in the snow, moaning and didn't want to go on. Somehow we made it to the top of the hill, Clyde refused to go any further. When we finally got home, cold and snowy, the folks were shocked that we had left Clyde in the snow.

Mom got her horse and set out after him. She found him where we had left him, he was so miserable, he didn't want to move and he didn't care if he was cold. Mom put him on the horse and got back to the ranch as fast as she could. For a long time Clyde was desperately sick. When my Dad learned about the cookies, he wouldn't let Clyde have water. Poor Clyde, he must have had a fire in his insides, he burped carbide flavored burps. He eventually got well, probably killed any worms he might have had, but he was a skinny boy ever after.

We all went back to school after Clyde had recovered. More people had left town as the mining slowed down. There were a lot of empty houses, which we explored. If they were locked and windows barred, we usually found a way underneath and usually there was some access to the house.

We looked through rooms, sometimes there was a lot of good junk such as someone's old spectacles or partly broken dishes. No one was kind enough to leave a fortune when they departed. The empty houses were spooky, though and we crept about on tiptoe, scaring ourselves.

We were all invited to a party. I didn't want to go as my shoes were boy's shoes and plenty worn. We scoured through our clothes and I found a pair of girl's slippers, none of us knew how they got there. We had never seen them before, but they just fit me, so I went to the party after all. There was a big cake and ice cream, and each of us won a gift, by winning a game. I won a pair of pepper and salt shakers, very small and pretty. I still have them.

Finally, Spring came, we could ride to school again. We saw that Casey's had built a new house. Mrs. Casey took us all through it;

An Unusual Childhood

we had stopped on our way home. She gave us some cookies, and we left. We did stop at their barn and looked around in it, but there was nothing but a harness and pack rat nests.

Those pack rats, sometimes called trade rats, were a nuisance and sometimes funny. One night one got into the house. We first knew about it when he got in the cupboard among the pans, and started them crashing and falling to the floor. Everyone was wakened. We all ran downstairs. Our parents were trying to corner the rat behind the range. They were in long nightgowns, there were pans fallen out of the cupboard, and the rat was darting about.

My Dad had the broom after him, and told us to not let him in the living room. We had a wood box, with caster wheels under it, for easy moving. The pack rat took refuge under the wood box. Mom ran to keep him from going into the living room, the rat ran for the door at the same time. Mom screamed as the rat ran under her feet, she lost her balance, and fell in the doorway. She just sat there and yelled, till Daddy pulled her to her feet. There was the unfortunate rat, dead in the doorway. Mom had sat on him and killed him.

All of us were laughing, except Mom; we stopped laughing when we saw the look on her face. We looked for what ever the rat had brought to trade, but didn't find anything.

Another time, a rat had some sort of pan; we were all in bed, when he climbed up to the eaves at the corner of the house, banging the pan all the way. At the roof, he would drop his load, and it went clanging to the ground. He would go down again, get the pan and noisily climb up again, only to drop the pan once more. This went on, over and over, until one of our parents went out and scared the rat away and brought the pan in.

We admired these honest rats; they always left something in place of what they took, even though the value was not always even. Usually they had their nests in rocks or old buildings. Most of their nests were of old sticks, with a few rags and sometimes a shiny object they had traded for.

Many of Jardine's people began to get autos instead of cars.

Harlene Jessie Reeves

Our neighbors had a Velie, a high-priced car. They had two boys and a girl, Audrey. Audrey had lots of pretty clothes and a tricycle. She had lots of dolls, but was mean to them. She and I played together and when Audrey found out I especially like her baby doll, she took the poor thing's clothes off and poured dirt on it.

We didn't know how that family seemed to have more money than others, till we found out the father had a moonshine still. Maybe it was the one we had found. One night that family was coming home from Gardiner, their nice car got on fire and burned completely up.

In another family, the father was superintendent of mines; he bought a car. They had a girl our age, another girl who was away at college and an older boy. He was the first person to be killed in a car accident in Jardine. We liked Louise, the girl our age. She had everything she wanted, but liked to do the things we did. She thought we had an exciting life.

Harlene with one of the Reeves' cows.

Once, on a weekend, Louise got to go home with us. There was still some snow, so Mom told us we could eat our lunch under a big tree where there was no snow. We were almost through eating when Mom saw a dead, dried-up bird. She told Louise to look at it, Louise lost her appetite.

81

An Unusual Childhood

It wasn't the bird's fault, he probably had been asleep when all the other birds went south, and when he woke up, it was too late because he didn't know the way. Anyway, we decided we liked Louise even if she was a pantywaist.

We started walking to school, it didn't seem far anymore, and our teacher was so accustomed to our being late, she just adjusted to it. School was out soon, anyway.

We had to work to help Mom plant the garden, and cut up potatoes to plant. Mom would plow a furrow and we dropped the cut pieces in. Then Mom plowed the other direction, making the dirt fall over and cover the potato pieces.

The cows and their new calves were turned out on the range and the horses we weren't using were turned into the horse pasture. Daddy went to work in Yellowstone Park.

The ants had taken over Grandma's hot bed, so we stayed away from it. We still had to weed the garden and go after cows, and we had to milk them. It seemed like we had more work, but still lots of time to wander all over our own place, and Teddy's Hill, Porcupine Jim, and through the horse pasture almost to Grey Donkey.

Later on, Mrs. Jones with Earl, Helen and Ruby came to stay for awhile. They didn't like Gardiner in the summer. Earl had joined the Boy Scouts and liked to show off his learning.

After the Jone's had gone back, we went all over, our cows seemed to go further, too. Many nights it would be dark and we had to stop and listen for a faint jingle when a cow moved her bell. It was a good thing we knew all their favorite places and where there were rocks to stumble over.

We didn't often ride after the cows, as the dumb things would often run through brush and under low limbs; the horses didn't want to follow, or we would get hit in the face by branches. After milking, we had to run the separator, to remove the cream from the milk. There was lots of warm foam on the skim milk, we

Harlene Jessie Reeves

liked to put it on bread and eat it. How awful it seems now!

Once, when the wheel of the separator was still running after the separating was through, I put my finger on the revolving center and somehow the gear wheel caught my hand and cut my thumb almost completely from my palm. Mom washed it in lye soap, poured some kerosene over it and wrapped it back in place. Aside from a scar, it healed up with no trouble. I felt quite important for awhile.

We had to build fence as our cows had gone into Parker's place. We were putting up a pole fence when Jim Parker came by. He gave us advice but no help, even though it was part of his, but the cows couldn't get out there, again.

We explored up Eagle Creek as far as old Sullivan's shack. It was a good thing he had been taken away to a veteran's home as he would have frozen for sure. His shack was made of branches, old sacks and other junk. We never knew what happened to poor old Sullivan.

Sylvia had started collecting pretty cards, valentines, and candy boxes. The boys and I decided to have a museum, in the boy's room. We fixed some shelves with boards and loaded them with bones, pretty rocks and the dried hooves of the colt that had died so long ago. We had a lot of arguments with Sylv, she thought our museum stunk. We thought her books and boxes were a mess.

That summer, I sat on a rock, not noticing a big bumble bee. I felt him, though.

One night, the boys went after the cows. The cows had gone a long ways, and a sudden storm came up. The boys were avoiding big trees because of lightning, when a bolt struck a stump, right in front of them. It started a fire, but the rain came down in torrents, and put the fire out. It was close to Perry's grave. The boys came all the way home. We had to let the cows go that night, so they came home by themselves the next morning.

That summer, we had a letter from Aunt Rene, one of Mom's sisters. She had four boys and one girl, but her smallest boy had got-

An Unusual Childhood

ten killed. Her letter said he had run out and tried to catch a ride on a wagon going by, he had slipped and fallen under the wagon and the wheel ran over his head. We didn't know him, but felt bad about it.

We had chicken that day for dinner and two of us pulled the wishbone, and one of the wishes was, "I wish Darrell didn't die." Aunt Rene was very religious, so took the loss for her boy quite bravely.

That summer, the boys caught a rabbit. They had it on a stump, where they skinned and dissected it. To our surprise, it had a lot of little rabbits inside. We were sorry about the baby rabbits, as they had died, too.

We were pretty excited when Daddy came home; he had bought a car—a Model T Ford. He showed Mom how to drive it. There were pedals on the floor for shifting gears and braking. It was black, and had a back seat. There was a gas tank under the front seat.

When it needed gas, the driver had to get out, take the seat out and the gas was put in--there was no gas pump, the car ran well going down hill, but going uphill, the gas didn't get to the motor and the Model T would start coughing and slowing down. We got used to waiting for it to almost stop, and we would jump out and push it up and over the hill, where it took off fast.

The Barnum and Bailey Circus came to Livingston. We got up real early, got our work done, and started to the Circus. It was sixty miles, and a washboard road all the way. We had to stop a lot, Daddy fixed things on the car, and we got out and snooped along the road and through people's pastures. It seemed forever to get to Livingston.

We were in time, though, the parade was going on, elephants holding each other's tails and fancy wagons, with all kinds of wild animals in cages. They all went into a huge tent. We got in and at the entrance we could touch the elephants.

It was a 3-ring circus. There were things going on in all three rings at the same time. There were ladies with hardly any clothes on, swinging on ropes at the top of the tent, clowns and people selling popcorn.

There was music and dancing ponies; and some fat people sitting in front of us so we couldn't see everything. After the show, we went through the side shows where we saw the fattest lady in the world, and the tallest man. There was a tattooed man that was tattooed so much he didn't need many clothes because he had so many colors on him, already.

We saw a lady get into a box and a lid was shut on her and a man stabbed the box clear through from every side and in the top with long, sharp knives. Then, he took all the knives out of the box, opened the lid and the lady got out, she wasn't hurt a bit.

Bud in front, Harlene and Clyde

Then we saw the littlest man and lady in the world. They were about as tall as a six-year old child, but were really grown-ups, the man had a mustache. The scariest thing was some wild men in a cage. We had to pay a nickel to see them, and went on a platform around their cage; they had wild, bushy hair with feathers in it, and wore nothing but short pants. They were brown-skinned and they leaped and screamed at us and made awful noises, scared us out in a hurry! My Dad was laughing at them.

All the way home we practiced the wild men's screams and the lion's roar. Our car made a lot of noise so it didn't bother our folks when we screamed and roared. We got home late that evening, but were up early, practicing "wild man."

An Unusual Childhood

We roared and screamed, and climbed up on the roof of the buggy shed, where Daddy had put some long pipes away, and discovered we could roar in one end of the pipe to someone at the other end, and it sounded just like lions. We ran through the cow pasture, with leaves in our hair, yelping and screaming like wild men. Mom told us how her older brother, Charlie, had scared her and her sisters with talks of the Wild Man of Borneo. Finally Daddy had his fill of the wild men, and we had to tame down.

The haying time had come again, this time Burl had to help fork the hay up on the wagon, and we had the usual tramping job, thistles and all. We especially hated the meadow, or wild hay, it had more thistles and other stickers. We were continually pulling stickers out of our tough, dirty feet.

Mom had sent to Sears Roebuck for bib overalls for all of us. Sylv and I didn't like them, the shoulder straps rubbed our shoulders and the bib part rubbed our fronts. We were beginning to have different shapes than our brothers.

I hated it; I hunted four leaf clovers and made wishes that I would turn into a boy.

The day came when it was back-to-school. That meant we had to get our horses, Daddy had shod them, we fought over the favorite saddle, and had new clothes from Sears Roebuck. We got a box of pears from Aunt Rene in Yakima. We had the long ride, again; it was enjoyable at first, the weather was nice, cold in the mornings but sunny and just right during the day.

On the way home, Clyde found a moose horn, it was a big one, so he took it behind him on the horse. It stabbed the horse, and made him buck. In spite of all the trouble, we managed to get that horn home. At noontime, we were hungry enough to eat anything. The box of pears didn't last long, we practically inhaled them.

As the colder weather came, Mom and Daddy came to Jardine, too. I don't remember what arrangements Daddy made for feeding our cows and horses at the ranch.

Harlene Jessie Reeves

Casey's had moved away, and we went through their house. It was a nice house, and seemed a shame for it to be empty. We noticed more houses empty in Jardine.

When the snows started, the Elk hunters started arriving. Mom had a good idea, the arsenic eater family had moved away, leaving their house empty. Mom got cots, and bedding, and put the cots in the rooms.

All the hunters were trying to find a place to sleep and eat, so Mom and Laura R. cooked for them. Our table was stretched full-length and Mom made stews, biscuits, soup, and anything. Those men were complementary and ate a lot. Mom rented cots to them, and they were willing to pay anything she asked.

Meat was no problem, as some of the hunters didn't care to take their elk home, they only wanted the antlers. One man even wanted the brains cooked. He sawed off the top of the elk's skull, dished out the brains, and Mom cooked them in a frying pan with eggs.

One day after school we saw Clyde coming home, he had a huge, fat man in tow. Mom said something about Clyde bringing home the bacon. He turned out to be one of the best customers we had. All the hunters ate at our lengthened table and told each other big lies about their former hunting adventures.

We enjoyed this part of the year. Laura R. teased Sylvia about a gawky, red-faced teenage boy that was hunting with his Dad. Our Dad didn't like her teasing, and it embarrassed Sylv.

School was about the same, and we had a Flexible Flyer sled, which we had to share. The schoolhouse hill became so slippery from sledding that we had to approach it from a different route.

One day, Burl and I were going down the hill double on the sled, when Jerry F., one of the miners, started across the street, we yelled at him as we were going too fast to stop, but he was slightly deaf, and didn't look our way. We hit him, knocked him down on top of us, and then he rode to the bottom of the hill. We were afraid we were in real trouble, but when we came to a stop, he got off, and with out a word, started back up the hill to his destination. I think he secretly enjoyed his ride.

As the year went on, there were more empty desks, as more people moved away and the mines closed down. I guess the big pay streak was running out. We were settled in the house in Jardine and Mom came there part-time. It snowed over and over, only the main streets (roads) were open.

We decided to climb to the top of one of the ridges, to gather some evergreens, a leafy plant that didn't lose its leaves in the winter. The leaves would make a nice Christmas trimming. As we got up the hill part way, we discovered the snow was so deep we had to throw ourselves full length on top of it, crawl until we sank down, and then flop on top, again. It was hard work and we were too warm, but we finally got to the evergreen leaves.

After we broke a few handfuls off, we went downhill, mainly by rolling and sliding. We came down faster than we climbed up. So, we had shiny evergreens, which we put somewhere and forgot about them.

We discovered that a dried elk hide made a perfect sled. We dragged it uphill, and turned it hair-side-down. Several of us held up the down hill edge, and when the hair was flat, away it would go. It was easy to stop, all we had to do was turn the skin so the hair was reversed and it would stop.

Mom and Daddy had to go back to the ranch, but we were more able to look after ourselves.

Sylvia made a friend with Edna Webster, and when they moved away, the two girls swore to write to each other.

It was plenty cold and I found somewhere a man's black over-coat. It came to my ankles, and I had a Paul Revere hat to go with it. Sylv stopped by Mrs. Koontz and Mrs. K told her I was very smart to wear my warm outfit, Sylv didn't think much of it, but I enjoyed the horrible get up.

Harlene Jessie Reeves

We had a new cookbook. We all learned to cook, at least one recipe. Sylv usually made gingerbread and rice, Burl made cupcakes and other cakes. I made rolls; Clyde wasn't interested in cooking, though he could fry eggs real well.

One night after school, we saw a column of black smoke up Bear Creek. Some men went to see what it was, and came back; soon the town was hearing all sorts of rumors. It was true that the Joe Tripple cabin had burned down and his body was in the ruins. It was said a murderer was about. We were scared stiff and decided to go home to the ranch.

The only problem was the cold and deep snow. We tried going on the Jardine-Gardner road, but a man whose name I can't remember, wouldn't let us go by his house, it was the last house on the edge of town. He told us to go back.

We finally climbed the hill above his house, and in spite of the deep snow, we got past it. He yelled at us but we went on, plowing our way through the snow. After we got well past his house, we slid down to the road. We had out-witted the old fool who was trying to keep us from freezing to death.

We hadn't gone far along the road when we met Mom, on her horse. We told her about the murdered man and his burned cabin, but she made us go back. When we passed the man's house, he came out and told Mom how he had tried to keep us from leaving town. Anyway, it turned out okay as Joe Tripple had shot himself after setting his own cabin on fire. His burned gun was found beside his body. Anyway, we went back to the ranch for awhile, where we ate like pigs.

The snow was really deep, over the fences and crusted on top. We hated to go back to school. The schoolhouse on the hill had been closed and we were moved to a small house. It had been someone's home at one time, it was a three bedroom house, our teacher lived in two rooms and we held school in the larger one. Our class had dwindled down to nine pupils, five of them Reeves. Sylv and I were 8th grade, and the oldest students. We were all grades in one room, one teacher.

An Unusual Childhood

It was interesting. Sylv and I had a hard time listening to the younger students making mistakes, but it was none of our business, even if it was our brothers. Bud didn't like the teacher; he would clam up and not answer her. She would shake him and get him by the chin and demand him to answer, but he would just stare blankly at her. Roy M. was the other second grader, so he got to answer when Bud wouldn't. Roy had forgotten he was a dog and was doing well in school.

Spring came and we went home in the Model T. We had a poor start. Something was wrong with the car, it sputtered but wouldn't start. My Dad was cranking it, while Mom moved the gas lever, but still it wouldn't start. Someone came by and asked if Dad had checked the gas tank. That meant removing the seat, and opening the cap to the tank. We were in the back and were lined up peering over the back of the front seat.

My Dad couldn't see in the tank, and not ever having experience with gas, he lit a match and held it over the opening, trying to see in. We didn't know at first what had happened--there was a roar, and a huge flame; red, orange and yellow, went up, burning our eyelashes and eyebrows, singing our front hair. The tank split open and took off into the air. My Dad had a fast sunburn and loss of eyebrows, too.

There weren't many neighbors around but the few that were there gathered quickly. We were all laughing, not knowing what an escape we had. So, we found that gas and matches are a poor mixture. We had to get another gas tank before we went home.

The ranch looked better every spring, mostly because of homesickness, but there was a lot of work to do, before we could leave for the ditch digging project. The cow barn had to be cleaned and the cows let out on the range, again. Most of the horses were frisky and had to be used again until they learned who was boss. During this time, Dot's foal was old enough to start riding. She was like a dog and seemed too easy to train.

One day some young men, they were actually teenagers, came to visit. Mainly they wanted to ride horses. Our folks arranged

Harlene Jessie Reeves

for them to ride our most dependable horses; Pat, Dot and Lady. We were told where to ride, Sylvia on Toots, Burl or Clyde on Rock. I rode Dot's filly. We went through the horse pasture, up over the ridge of Grey Donkey, and down the other side. We had never been there before; it was a hangout for wild horses. It had a lot of small meadows and a creek.

On our way back, my filly, suddenly shied unexpectedly, then began to buck straight downhill. I finally lost my grip and landed in the sage brush while my horse went on bucking and plunging down the hill. I tried to catch her, and Sylv and my brothers went after her on their horses. Our guests sat on their horses and watched the useless chase, we couldn't get near her.

It was nearing dark so the guests wanted to get back. One of them insisted that I get on Dot behind him; I wanted to walk, as I saw my brothers grinning. I knew they were going to tease me. I rode behind on Dot and was as stiff as a cement block. I was worried about the runaway horse, and the teasing I would get. When we got home, our parents didn't say much until our visitors left, and we sure got told off for leaving the filly.

Early next day our parents went in search for her. They found where she had stopped to drink and followed her trail to where a bunch of wild horse tracks were. They were all mixed up. I wonder what the wild ones thought when they met one of their own kind, wearing a saddle and bridle.

One or the other of our parents went looking for her, nearly every day, finally giving up as there were other things to do. My Dad went to work in the Park, and Mrs. Jones with Helen, Ruby and Earl came to stay for awhile. Earl was thirteen and my brothers looked up to him. Mom had learned to herd the car and often used it instead of horses.

One warm day she left for Gardiner, Sylv and I and the Jones girls, and Mrs. Jones stayed home. My brothers and Earl took off on a project of their own.

It was one of the worst days of our lives.

91

An Unusual Childhood

The boys went off wandering. They happened to take the road toward Gardiner, and turned on the branch road to Jardine. Some people had lived there for awhile, but had left their place to the pack rats. It was a small house beside a small stream with lots of willows and the type of rock formation that rattle snakes had their headquarters in. It was a perfect set-up for snooping for interesting things.

In the house, there wasn't much, but in one of the cupboards was a baking powder can, and in the can was a small copper object that looked like a 22 Caliber bullet. The boys all examined it closely, trying to figure out what it was. It didn't have the right shape for a bullet, yet it was the right size, though longer. Finally they decide to break it open to find out what was inside. Burl put it on a rock, and holding it with his left hand, pounded it with another rock.

There was a terrific explosion, rocks and dirt flew, and after the dirt settled the startled boys could hardly see, but they saw enough to head for home three miles away. Earl was unhurt, but Burl's and Clyde's knees and Burl's eyes had dirt and gravel in them and worst of all, Burl's left hand was gone. It was bleeding pretty bad and a long walk home, so Earl used his handkerchief and Scout knowledge, and put a tourniquet on it and wrapped the bloody mess in another handkerchief, and they all headed home. It must have been a terrible walk, but they finally reached the road going to ours and Parker's place. Here they were lucky, Jim Parker came along in his Ford T.

He stopped and heard the boys' story. He didn't really believe Burl was badly hurt, so he took off the bloody handkerchief. One look at the mangled flesh and bones, and Jim P. re-wrapped it, and got Burl and Clyde in his car and headed for Gardiner. He hadn't gone far when he met Mom on her way home.

The boys were transferred to our car, and Mom made the fastest trip back to Gardiner where she could phone Daddy. I don't know all the details, but somehow, the boys were taken to Livingston as there were no doctors in Gardiner. Burl had surgery and had to stay in the hospital, but Clyde's knees were cleaned and he came home.

92

Harlene Jessie Reeves

Burl was in the hospital for quite awhile, we got to go and see him. Thank goodness for Mrs. Jones and Earl. Earl actually had saved Burl's life. When Burl finally got to come home, Mom had a lot of bandages and they had showed her at the hospital how to put clean dressings on the stump that once was a hand.

We were shocked, but Burl was quite casual about it. He told us he was going to call the stub hand, "Judd," which he did. After it healed and became strong, he would pound things and do anything the rest of us could with "Judd". It has never kept him from doing anything that anyone else can do.

Sometimes we had a few pigs; they were kept in a pen and drank all the skim milk. My Dad fixed a stove pipe, funnel fashion so we could pour the milk in the pipe top and it ran into the pigs' trough. That way they couldn't get in the way and have milk baths. One pig didn't grow, so he was let out to eat grass.

He still didn't look well and seemed eternally hungry. He was a pest, at first we thought he was cute, but later he became a nuisance. He was always running and squealing at our heels. We would try to creep silently out the door but he seemed to be on the alert at all times, he would appear; squealing and running behind us. We couldn't out-run him any way we tried.

One evening, Burl and I were going after the cows, and that stupid pig fell in line, grunting and squealing. One of us, picked up a stick, and clubbed the pig over the back, hoping to chase him away. Instead, the pig dropped in his tracks, kicking. We were sure he was dying, especially when he managed to get his front legs in gear and dragged himself away, his back legs helpless.

We went on (no pig behind us) and got the cows in, but we were sure we were in trouble. When we came back to the barn with the cows, we were met by the idiot pig, running on all fours and squealing as well as ever. We sure were glad to meet him.

Later that summer, the Model T developed a knock and Mom got the instruction book out. It seemed something was wrong with the gears. So, Mom got under it and removed some bolts or

An Unusual Childhood

something, and it turned out to be the oil pan and it had a lot of oil in it as well as some gear teeth. One of the gears had broken teeth and had caused more gears to break teeth off. Mom set the oil to one side and got the gears. She saw she would have to go to Gardiner for parts, which reduced her back to horse and buggy, so took most of the day.

She got back, and early next day, started putting the Model T back together. When she went to replace the oil pan, the oil was gone. Our sickly pig had drunk it. So Mom had to go back to town again, muttering her opinion of the pig. It seemed to be the answer to the pigs problem, he began to grow and fatten, and soon was a good, fat pig. He was no bother to us anymore, and joined his mates in the pig pen. We never told our parents of our clubbing the pig.

Our Dad built a garage for the Model T. We kept all kinds of things in the garage, the car sat in the yard. The garage had a small attic, it was hard to get into, we had to climb the walls and scramble over the rafters to get to it for a secret hide-away. The hideaway was known to our parents and Sylv, still we thought it was secret. All the snooping into empty houses made it easy for us to get into the attic.

It was haying time again, and at every harvest, there were lots of field mice. We caught some and made a cage for them, keeping it a secret from Mom. We managed to get the cage and the mice up into the garage attic. Every day, we took bread, or oats, and water to them. They didn't seem to eat much. We visited them a lot, then sometimes only two times a week.

Finally, we forgot all about them. It was quite awhile before we remembered the captives and we took some bread, expecting to see all the mice, starving to death. We got to the garage and got a shock! There was only one mouse there; he was the biggest, fattest, bright-eyed mouse we had ever seen. There was no sign of the others. The big one sat up and stroked his whiskers. He was proud and vain. We named him "Mousie Crusoe", and sentenced him to death for cannibalism. He was caught and brought down where he faced a jury of cats who declared him guilty and finished him off.

Poor Mousie Crusoe!

94

Harlene Jessie Reeves

Every summer we kept a look-out for our lost horse with the saddle and bridle, we were told of her being seen by others, the saddle hanging under her, but no one seemed to be able to catch her. Finally we forgot all about her. Somewhere in those mountains, is a weather-beaten saddle and bridle. They were worth more than the horse.

Some people arrived that summer; they wanted a spirited, but gentle horse for a lady to ride. They drove a big Lincoln car, with a windshield between the passenger's and their uniformed chauffeur. The only horse they wanted was Dot, in spite of her bum foot.

Mom asked me if I wanted to sell her, which I didn't, so I named a huge price, $50.00. They peeled off $50.00 without a blink, I was shocked, horses were worth $10--$15.00 dollars at that time. I wanted to back out, but Mom told me I had to keep my word.

Later the people sent a trailer and I told Dot good-bye. I had $50.00 but no horse. I went upstairs and back in a closet and bawled till I couldn't cry anymore. Later, Mom told me I could have Patsy, she looked a lot like Dot, but was younger and not broken.

We started breaking Patsy. I rode her, she was tied to the saddle on Mom's horse, but she sure could buck, anyway. We started for Jardine, and I was thrown off in the sagebrush over and over. Patsy was pretty tired by the time we came to the steep mountain, and behaved quite well.

When we got to the Jardine road, there was a car, and patsy put on a show for the people, by bucking down the bank and throwing me in the dirt. I didn't like Patsy too well, but she did finally become a good horse, but never could run like Dot.

It was nearing fall, so I got the Sears Roebuck catalogue and sent off an order, without Mom's permission. I ordered new pants for all the boys, clothes that Sylv wanted and material and skirts and two pairs of shoes for myself. It took nearly all my $50.00.

When the packages came to Jardine, we had to load two horses. Mom was shocked when she saw my shoes, one pair was light

An Unusual Childhood

blue slippers, and the other was boy's dress oxfords, I was tired of wearing high shoes, especially since half the time we couldn't find the button hook. Besides the button shoes were not in style anymore. I don't know why I got the slippers.

I used the rest of my money and bought a huge sack of bananas for a family in Gardiner. They had no Daddy and were dirty and hungry.

Our Dad got a job in Yellowstone Park; he was in charge of building Museums at several places. We got to go and camp at the Madison River camp, and met other people, but we had to go back to the ranch, and get ready for school. We decided to walk at first, one morning our brothers didn't get to school. That evening Burl explained to Mom that his pants had split before he got down the big hill, and strangely enough both Clyde's and Bud's had split, too.

Mom thought it a little odd, she talked to our teacher later and she laughed. She said they must have hated school to have to tear up their clothes. The boys were not too happy because Mom had told the teacher their embarrassing situation.

Finally the cold came and we were back on horseback. Patsy was a good horse by now. Later our parents moved back to Jardine, the carbide cookies had scared them. There were only nine pupils in the school, now—five Reeves, 2 Marchingtons, a Mary Louise, and a Louise.

Mary Louise was living with her grandparents and had a music box, she wanted to be called Louise, because Louise B. was the mining company's superintendent's daughter; but Mary Louise was fat and German-looking, while Louise B. wasn't fat and was a lot of fun in spite of her higher rank among the kids.

Mary Louise's grandpa was the one who tried to keep us from leaving town when we had the murder scare. He also was the one who sawed and cut the wood for us during the winter. We didn't like him.

This winter was like the last, we had the hunters again and

Harlene Jessie Reeves

Buffalo Flats was like a battle ground when the elk were surrounded. I was sorry for the elk, if they crossed the Park line to look for food, they were shot. If they stayed in the Park, it was higher and colder, so they starved.

Every year there were more hunters. Mom made more money off them than we earned on the Ranch. Our Dad was thinking about moving somewhere, where we could be close to a high school, Mom threatened we should be sent to a reform school mainly because we forgot to do our chores or set all the kettles to soak.

There were not a lot of people left in town, and not much to do so on Friday nights the people gathered in each other's homes and had parties. There was cake. Everyone who had a baby put them in one bed. They were all wrapped in their blankets and slept through all the noise. My Dad could play the fiddle and the grown-ups danced. It was always way late when everyone left, and we were tired out.

It seemed like these parties were often, and Mary M. giggled through all of them. School was the usual thing; I read every book in our school library. We got our free iodine tablets; the state was short of iodine in the soil. We also got little booklets about a boy who had a vaccination and lived, and another boy, whose mother wouldn't let her son have a vaccination, and he died of diphtheria. We never got a vaccination, though.

We got chicken pox and got to stay home. We spent most of the time reading Sears Roebuck. Burl, Clyde and I wished for skis. We wished out loud so much our Dad said we could order 3 pair. We chose six-foot-pine, cost a dollar-thirty-nine cents in the catalogue. We waited and watched all the time, chanting: "Six-foot pine, dollar-thirty-nine." We were still quarantined but not sick. When the skis finally arrived, we got them on in record time and out in the snow.

It was a warm day, we were careful to stay on the level, as it was quickly learned that we didn't know how to ski. School was in session, so naturally we made our way there. We walked our skis back and forth in front of the school windows, attracting the attention of our schoolmates. Finally the teacher could stand no more of our

An Unusual Childhood

parade and came out and told us to go home.

While we were out of school we practiced with our skis. We loved them, they were polished and waxed, and we got so we could go down-hill without falling. Burl even could jump, on small drifts. We didn't have ski poles and got along without them, very well. We took our skis with us when we went to the ranch, where we learned more.

The hardest part was going up-hill, but it was worth it to come down, again. Our Dad used snow shoes a lot in the winter, I tried them, but they were so wide it was hard to walk with the feet kept wide apart. Snowshoe tracks in the snow make a pretty design-like a strange, big bird had been walking about.

As spring neared, the snow got mushy during the day, the sun shone in a blue-green sky, but it would freeze up again at night. We could walk on top of the hard-crusted snow going to school, and pick our way through the watery slush when we came home. It seemed ages before all the snow left, and the new, green grass began to grow. We let our cows out to eat along Bear Creek, and around the empty homes.

Some people lived in a deserted part of town, and our cows came to visit them. No one knew these people very well, as they seemed to stay in their house most of the time. Once in a while, the Mrs. was seen shaking her dust mop outdoors.

One evening when we were bringing the cows home, she came out and screamed at us to keep our cows away. It was the first time we knew they had been there. There were horses around town that no one seemed to care if they ate in the empty yards and along Bear Creek.

We didn't say anything to the angry lady, but told our folks about it. The next day we were told to herd the cows past the un-friendly woman's house. She came out as we went by, and watched to be sure we were not going to leave the cows near her house.

We took our animals well past her place, and once they started eating, we left them and went back to school. That evening we went after the cows and brought them home with the angry woman watching. As we went by her house, she yelled, "Keep your cows away!" from hers.

This went on and we got tired of it, so one evening on our way after the cows, we stopped in front of her yard and invented a dance--we circled around in the road, and jumped up and down to the tune of "Keep your cows away, Ha! Ha! Ha!--Keep your cows away, Ha! Ha! Ha!"

We got action. The woman dashed in her house and then out again with a rifle. She was so mad, she couldn't shoot straight, but she meant to get herself

Naomi (Davis) Reeves

a Reeves kid or two. We left for home and my Dad went after the cows. He stopped to see the woman and we never knew what was said, but after that we took the cows past her house and returned them in the evening; no more excitement.

We were really happy to go back to the ranch, Jardine was not a pretty town, with the roads, houses and the big stamping mills and their piles of cast-off ore. Bear Creek was too rough to wade in, not like Eagle Creek. There was a wide spot in Eagle Creek, where the water wasn't deep and the bottom was covered with smooth pebbles. It was one of our favorite places on a warm day. We all went barefoot as soon as the weather was warm enough, it was rough at first, but by haying time our feet were pretty tough.

My Dad came home with a bookcase and a lot of books. I

An Unusual Childhood

read all of them and whenever I could corner my brothers, I would read to them, too. Sometimes I would get so interested in the book I would look up to discover my audience had crept away. They had been stricken with wheels in their heads.

My Dad had gotten them some toy iron Model T cars, so they built roads in a dirt bank, where they buzzed and "Ooo-gah-ed" endlessly. Progress had arrived. My Dad said Burl had wheels going around in his head.

Mom liked going places; she was always fixing the T.

Our museums were thrown out and Sylv's collection was reduced to a few rare items, such as empty candy boxes. She began to have nightmares. Many nights she scared me silly, she thought a gorilla was coming up the stairs and into our room. It seemed so real that I got scared, too, and we crawled into bed with Mom.

The folks planted a bigger field of potatoes and took out more sagebrush; I was big enough to drive a team over the newly plowed new land. We had a home-made drag—nothing more than a lot of branches, nailed between some planks. It smoothed over the rough spots and left a good, smooth field for planting. The main thing, there was no place to sit, and my legs got tired in a hurry.

Our ditch was partly dug across Teddy's hill, but wasn't connected to the one further away; we still had to get a way across Parker's place. My Dad had to work out so much he didn't get much done on the ditch. He was talking more about moving to where there was a high school. We thought it would be nice, until fall came with its beautiful weather and the bright-colored leaves.

Mom and we dug the potatoes and Mom sold them for $5.00 a sack, an unheard of price, but she was so tired she was sick for awhile. We were riding to school again, but it seemed different, the shadow of moving away made us appreciate the ride, the duck pond, Casey's Lake and even the steep hillside. Mom invited our teacher to visit over a week-end, and she fell in love with the ranch, she even like helping with the chores.

100

Harlene Jessie Reeves

Aunt Rene wrote more often, telling how wonderful the State of Washington was, the mild winters and the great crops of fruit and about every type of vegetables that could be grown. It seemed quite tempting, but my Dad had found out that Blanding's ranch was for sale. We really didn't want to leave the country, so he made arrangements to buy the Blanding ranch. He and Mrs. Blanding had some long talks trying to come to an agreement.

Meanwhile, school went on as usual. Christmas came and we had a few things, and besides the usual were long ropes of beads, they were all colors; and turned out to be candy. If we wore them very long, they got warm and sticky and left their color on our necks.

Daddy belonged to the Eagle's Club in Gardiner, and they arranged a New Year's dance. It was a masquerade, and Sylv wanted to go, as she felt quite grown-up. Mom made her a dress, it was fringed burlap, and we gathered all the beads we could get, including the colorful candy beads. She wore homemade moccasins, which Mom was clever at making.

Sylv had long, black hair, all she needed for a mask, was over her eyes. Even peering through the eye slits, she had brown eyes, perfect for an Indian Maiden. Mom braided her hair into two pigtails and made a bright band to wear around her head. Some colored feathers stuck in the head band, and Sylvia was a perfect Indian Maiden, so off to the dance she went with our parents.

Sylvia had never danced before, but she got by and was practically the belle of the ball. All the single, young men danced with her, they talked but she was silent as an Indian. When the New Year came in, masks came off. There were several embarrassed young men who had made a great attempt to attract a lovely young lady, only to discover they were wasting the evening with a school child.

When the awards were made, Sylvia got the first prize, earning many angry glares from eligible young women. Later, we learned that Aunt Sadie had been one of the judges, and in Sylv's mind, she had influenced the judging. In our eyes, she deserved the prize.

Back to school, it was getting harder, we were being readied for our state tests. In Montana, all eighth graders had to go to the county seat to take state exams before going on to the ninth, or Junior High. Sylv and I probably got extra teaching, as we were the only 8th grades, and our Mom and our teacher were friends.

Sylv was sick a lot that winter, but a lady who had been a nurse before she married, came and did all she could for Sylv. Meanwhile, Daddy was still negotiating for the Blanding ranch. We looked forward to moving into the big house.

It was plenty cold. Our Dad had a habit of teasing us by pinching our legs with his toes, we avoided him when he had his shoes and socks off. He was always doing something to make us laugh. One evening we were shivering around the heater, our Dad pulled one of his stunts: he could leap up in the air and kick his heels together before touching the floor.

This particular morning, he was trying to prove to us that the cold air was invigorating, he leapt up and kicked his heels together and yelling, "Yippee!", but when he came down he was too close to the bed frame. The sharp, iron corner caught one heel and cut a slice off it. He was pretty quiet after that, and it was a miserable thing to walk with. It was a good thing he did it during the winter, so it was healed up by summer, when the work started.

Negotiations were resumed, concerning the Blanding ranch, the Mrs. having settled on a price. She wanted a large down-payment, which was more than we could get all at once. So Daddy went to our old friend Mr. Scott. It seemed whenever we had an emergency, Mr. Scott came up with the money.

He was truly a friend. Mr. Scott loaned Daddy the down-payment for the ranch and Daddy came home in high spirits. The next day, we expected to be the new owners of the Blanding ranch. We did wonder about our own place, not yet realizing that our government would solve that problem.

Next day, Daddy left early. We kept watching the road and waiting for him to come back "with the papers." It didn't take long when we saw our car returning slowly home. When Daddy finally got home he was not as happy as we expected him to be. We were all questions, but he didn't want to say much.

It seemed that a well-to-do cattleman from Gardiner had been in to see Mrs. B. and offered her more money, so she tore up the agreement with our Dad and sold the place to Mike L. If our opinions caused pain, Mrs. B. and Mike L. must have suffered agony.

The problems of where we should go to school became closer as the school year ended. We would have like to have stayed where we were, but Aunt Rene kept writing those wonderful letters, and Daddy began to think of that opportunity. He was determined we should continue school. I'm sure Mom wanted to stay put, she had lived there nearly all of her life.

We quit thinking of the Blanding ranch and kept hoping my Dad would quit thinking of high school. In my mind it would be an ordinary school, with big high desks and everything else up high.

School was out and Sylvia and I had to go to Gardiner for the state tests. Mrs. Scott was nice enough that she invited us to stay with them as the tests took two days.

Mom had made new dresses for us and we left with clean underwear and new shoes. The folks went to Livingston on business, probably concerning our ranch. Sylvia and I were treated royally by the Scotts, I had been afraid of Mr. Scott, "Kind, old gentleman". He had a cane and his wheel chair, and his wife, who was much younger, looked after him as though he was really dear to her. We admired them.

Mrs. Scott showed us to our room, we were feeling like princesses, when we saw the beautiful room. It was carpeted, and the bed was all white and lacy. Then there was a bathroom, with a tub and wash basin and, of all things, a toilet, the first one inside of a house we had ever seen. It was an embarrassing thing to us, as Mrs. Scott showed us how to pull a chain and the entire contents of the thing disappeared with a mighty roar.

The next morning we had breakfast in a sunny windowed

An Unusual Childhood

room. Mrs. Scott had flowers on her table and all the dishes, cups and saucers matched. Even the silverware was all alike. Their house was across Yellowstone River, almost opposite Aunt Sadie's. While we were eating breakfast, we watched a group of deer across the river. They were eating and running about, practically in town.

We went to the school, it was not too far from Scotts, and I was not impressed by the building. It was a grey, concrete, square building, quite large in comparison to the Jardine school.

There were a lot of students, many were from Gardiner, others from small schools like ours. No one was very friendly; all worrying about the tests. One of the first things I did after getting a desk, test papers and so on, was the ink episode. Everyone had a fresh bottle of ink. I struggled with the cap on my bottle, it wasn't as tight as I expected and came off; dumping about half of the ink on the front of my new silk dress. I had to go down to the rest rooms and clean off the blue as best I could. The school rest rooms had modern facilities, too, and smelled pretty bad. It was a sure sign of civilization.

When the long tests were over, Sylvia and I went back to the Scotts. We were told that we would get our grades in the mail, so we had something to worry about for awhile.

We went to Aunt Sadie's and waited for our parents. Aunt and Uncle had bought a big, old-fashioned barn near their home, and they had changed it into a sort of rustic hotel. Gardiner was planning on a new bridge over Yellowstone River. More tourists came every year and a better bridge was needed. It would be built where the swinging bridge was.

So, Aunt and Uncle could see that in the future there would be a lot of people wanting rooms. We went through the re-built barn and were quit impressed. The stalls were converted into small rooms, all gaily decorated with new wallpaper, and bunches of paper flowers. There was a stairway going to the loft, it had been partitioned into rooms and with the largest one Aunt had really been carried away with ideas.

It was papered with pink rose paper, and there were some

Harlene Jessie Reeves

of Aunt's paintings on the walls. The window had fluffy curtains to match the bed. She told us it was the bridal suite; in fact it had that name above the door. I was thinking of horse bridles and sweetness, so I was somewhat confused, but didn't say anything.

Our folks came after us, and we went home. They had bought something for us in Livingston, but we had to wait till we got home to see what it was. We were quite unhappy about the gifts; the main ones I can remember were three pairs of lady's high-buttoned shoes that Mom had gotten for practically nothing at a rummage sale.

They though the shoes would surely fit three of us. The awful truth was that they were all one size and fit Clyde, but no one else. Clyde had the dangedest luck. He had to wear those shoes, they were even out of style for ladies. They did make pretty good cowboy boots if no one noticed the buttons. Somehow they were lost and rid of.

We had the shadow of not living there, it was a background: "If we move, better schools, etc.". We didn't get more horses to break, but still had lots to do.

Once my Dad got a brand new rope, it was good and long, and as new ropes come, it was raw cut on the ends. Daddy worked a long time, one end he braided in such a way, that it wouldn't un-ravel, in the other end he put a loop, weaving the un-braided ends backward to make a strong loop. It was a roping rope and we were all interested in seeing him use it. We were gathered at the front door of the house, and one of the horses was loose, grazing near the barn.

So, Daddy coiled his new rope and proudly showing his marksmanship, twirled the loop and sent it sailing. It coiled around the startled horse, she made a great leap and took off, around the parked mowing machine and away she went. The mower had neatly cut the new rope in half. We couldn't help but laugh. Daddy laughed too, but his heart wasn't in it.

We had a box camera, so we started taking pictures of our place. We went past the leaning rock and up onto the ridge, the horse pasture, and took pictures of a tree seemingly growing out of a rock,

105

and all of our outgrown teddy bears, my old doll among the wild flowers. There was a flat rock up there, I often wondered what it was, as it had several colors and was shiny, but way too big to try to dig up.

My Dad went back to work in the park. After the early work was done, Mom and all of us went to Gardiner where Mom took the lady with the dirty kids with us and we went to where Daddy was working for one day.

We each picked out one dirty kid to specialize in. They were cute kids, all with big brown eyes and not many brains. They were nice pets, but we got tired of them pretty fast, seemed like one of them was always bawling or had a runny nose. Mom got tired of them, too.

As the summer passed we were beginning to be aware that we might leave and never see the place again. We and the Parker family were the only ones still in that area. We never saw the Parkers, except my snoopy brothers spied on Geraldine and a boy friend and she scared the living daylights out of them with her threats.

One by one the ranches were bought by the Federal Government. They had a new group of young game managers who decided that there wasn't enough range and feed for the elk herds. To us it seemed to be a lot of grass, year after year it grew, dried up and wasn't used. It was thick and matted in the range area, but we were advised that we couldn't plan on staying there.

A new group came in with powerful machinery; they sawed up the big boulders, cut them into slabs and hauled them away. The slabs were made into granite grave markers. Somehow we didn't feel like the usual.

No haying was done, and we went more often to Yellowstone. We took more and more pictures, of the whole place, from the top of Grey Donkey Ridge. I noticed more, the view of Mammoth Hot Springs, and the flowers, the riot of colorful wild flowers, and late in the season, the bright fireweed. Our film wasn't in color, because it hadn't been developed, yet.

Harlene Jessie Reeves

One day, our Dad came home, and said he'd sold all the cows. They were taken away. The horses were turned into their pasture and we went to Yellowstone, where we stayed and met new people who were working on the museums.

We learned to make friends with new kids, and did no work, but lots of exploring. There were not a lot of people there and the bears were quite tame but not as bad as they would get years later. My Dad held out against the Government on selling our place, he was trying to find a place near the Park and yet had the school problem in mind.

We went home; fall was approaching with the wildly changing leaves and the beautiful Indian summer coming. One day, a hawk came down after one of our chickens. The fool chicken had gotten under the chicken wire that Mom had over her flowers to keep the chickens out. The lucky hen couldn't get out of the wire and the hawk went in after her. We heard the racket, and ran outside. Mom got a potato sack and managed to get the hawk in it.

The hysterical hen got out and ran for the hen house, of course, she forgot what she was running from and resumed her scratching and picking about half way there. So, we owned a hawk.

Mom or Daddy had tried to shoot a hawk, they would sit in the bare top of the tall spruce trees and seemed to have guardian angels as they were hard to hit. Our Dad told the park people about our hawk and they made a trade with Mom. She got the worst of it--she got a stuffed Kingfisher bird, mounted on a stick, it had feathers and sat and stared in every home our folks had.

Finally came the day our Dad came home and told us he had made the agreement to sell. He had no choice; our government condemned our place and told him how much they would pay him for it. We (Fools!) were happy to go to a new place. We sold most of our horses and furniture to a dude ranch. Our white-faced bull was one of the last to go, he was tied between two horses and our folks dragged him all the way to Gardiner. Poor thing, he knew a bad deal when he saw it.

107

An Unusual Childhood

Daddy decided we would have to get another car to haul our belongings. We were to go to the land of Eden: Yakima, Washington, where Aunt Rene kept telling us how wonderful it was: "Praise the Lord." Aunt Rene had been married twice and had a girl and three boys and a new baby expected. We were eager to see them. We spent a lot of time in Gardiner, where we looked over the supply of new cars, two of them. They were the latest, had their gas tank in back and a hand-operated gear shift. We sat in a Ford and practiced shifting gears. Mom visited friends; some people here gave us a police dog, Nickodemus.

Our Dad finally bought a '28 Chevrolet in Livingston, and we cheerfully loaded all we could get into the two cars. Fall had really set in, and just before we left, some friends came and they stayed over-night, and in the morning found their car frozen up. There was some delay, but we finally left, Mom driving the T and Daddy the Chevy. We were really excited.

I, at least never looked back as we drove over the bridge and up the lane.

A few snow flakes were coming down and our house sat, empty of people but still holding part of the furniture and clothes, as there was a limit to what we could have. I never looked back to Gray Donkey, Teddy's Hill or anything. We had enough to go on; our clothes, cookware, and the big teddy bear Mom had made for Clyde out of badger fur. We left our skis in the garage, our stoves, our bookcase full of books, our farm machinery, all buildings, the house, barn, blacksmith shop, buggies, and the fancy Surrey with the fringe on top—everything that the dude ranch didn't need.

By the time we got to Gardiner, there was a real snow storm going, so my Dad chose what he thought was a Southerly route. It turned out to be a longer route, and what was worse, it was a high altitude, where winter was well under way. We couldn't travel fast, so had to stop for nights, we had not planned on this expense.

The worst place was Ashton, Idaho, well before we got there, the snow was piling up and the Model T quit. Our folks left it, where it quit, and we all went on in to Ashton, where we stayed in a new motel, built one board thick, and the roof leaking like mad.

The folks found an axle for the Model T, and went back to fix it. Then Clyde got pretty sick, so we stayed in that miserable place and got a case of homesickness started. Also, our hoard of money began to dwindle.

The snow was coming down so thickly we could hardly see the road, and I, for one, wondered what kind of mistake we were making. People were not friendly and it seemed the road went on forever.

We finally made it over the mountains and met flat country, where the trees were leafless and the wind blew. We stayed at a little town called Mountain Home, where there was no snow, yet and the orchards and evergreen trees met in friendly lines. It was rolling hill country and pretty. Then on we went to Yakima.

It was desolate looking country, flat land, and grey with the coming winter. We had a motel at the next stop, with gas heat and a range. It was the first time we had seen gas heaters, they were fantastic, one turned a handle and held a lighted match over the burner plate, and, like magic, a blue flame sprang to life, no smoke, even.

Part of our journey followed the old Oregon Trail of the covered wagon days, the ruts made by the wagons still there, in places. We finally came to a stretch of road that lay flat, one could see ahead for miles and the road lay ahead as far as we could see. There was a sign that read the speed limit, "100 MPH, Fords do your best!" Our cars were no problem, at 30 MPH we were speeding. This was new, raw farmland and under a new irrigation system.

There was no snow; the land looked deserted and un-friendly. We drove for hours before coming to the Columbia River. There was a toll bridge across the River to the opposite side. We went across and downhill on the bridge, where the station sat, a lady in it, to collect money. Daddy was driving the T, and the brakes had gone bad, so he had a hard time getting stopped, going by the Toll house.

The girl popped out of the toll house, screaming, "Stop,

An Unusual Childhood

Stop!" as the Model T whizzed by. My Dad was mad, he yelled at her, "I am!" and continued down the road, finally getting the T under control. We didn't help matters much as we paid our toll, and as Mom drove on, we chanted, "Stop! Stop!" at the angry girl. We were all tired and ready for a fight.

In fact, we did fight, not very pleasant for our tired drivers. We finally made it to Yakima, where we drove around trying to find Aunt Rene's in a strange and busy town. We finally did find their house in the outskirts of the town, surrounded by orchards.

We were startled to see apples laying on the ground, and a few still hanging in the leafless trees, but soon discovered that they weren't good to eat. Aunt Rene came running to Mom, they hadn't seen each other for years, and Rene was so weepy it took awhile to get her story. We were looking for our cousins, but the only one present was not born, yet.

He made our Aunt look very odd, as she was so thin. It seemed that her family had just moved into their house as their former one had just burned down. After moving, all our cousins came down with Typhoid fever, and were in the county hospital. Bennie not expected to live, though the others were doing well.

No wonder Aunt was so glad to see Mom. We heard her story; she hadn't been home when their house caught fire. Virginia had just made a cake, and in the excitement of the burning building, Virginia saved the cake, but threw it over the yard fence, where some geese ate it.

When our new Uncle came home, we met him for the first time. He was selling McNess products and not being successful, as the depression had already hit Yakima. Uncle was a mild man, with a sturdy build and comfortably big tummy like Santa Claus.

We were quite impressed with him, as he brought a sack as big as a spud sack full of bread. After supper, that evening, we just had to go see our sick cousins. Aunt and Uncle came also, to direct the way and to visit their family. It seemed a long way, we'd had plenty of riding.

Harlene Jessie Reeves

When we got to the hospital, we couldn't go into the room where all our cousins were, but Aunt Rene told them who we were and they were feeling so much better that they were anxious to see us. They all said hello, and sat up in their beds to stare at us, except Bennie. He didn't seem to notice anyone telling him to say hello. Finally a tiny squeak came from him, making Aunt very happy, as he had made no responses to anything since he'd first gotten sick.

We stayed at Rene's, while my Dad contacted agencies, looking for a good farm. We were a good thing for our Aunt and Uncle, as they were very poor, having lost everything in the fire, and Uncle out of work. The McNess products didn't sell well, as most people weren't buying any more than they had to.

We were sorted for beds and Sylvia and I went to sleep in a strange bed, in a strange house, in a strange country. Now and then a car drove by on the road in front of the house, and during the night, a train went by leaving a long, lonesome whistle off in the distance. I had already changed my mind about leaving Montana.

The winter went on, but there was no snow, the cousins recovered and were brought home, except for Bennie. He was better, but terribly weak. The table was stretched to its greatest length with all the kids and four grown-ups. We had enough to eat because Aunt had canned and preserved everything that was grown in this valley. Our ranch money dwindled, as our Dad felt we should do our share, and Uncle continued bringing the sacks full of bread, $1.00 per sack.

He told us that when he got rich, he was going to buy a piano for Virginia. She was thin and had a long, thin face. She considered herself well above us country kids. She wore make-up and high-heeled shoes and had never been on a horse in her life. We like Monty and Winfred, except Winfred did anything he pleased, being the youngest.

Finally Bennie could come home, he looked like all bones and skin, with huge brown eyes. He was still very weak and we felt sorry for him because he could hardly do anything. Virginia pitied him and vowed she would take care of him.

111

An Unusual Childhood

It wasn't long, though that Bennie was doing all the low jobs, peeling potatoes, doing dishes and mopping the floor. Aunt's baby was born and named Charlie. There were diapers and more work, and Bennie was assigned to most of them. Monte had pigeons in an old barn on their place; he said whenever he went near them that they said, "Look at the coon!"

We didn't go to school that winter, as we were so far behind, and our folks were looking for a farm. They were getting tired of the huge family, Bennie's problems and Uncle getting drunk on McNess vanilla. He was his best customer. The longer we stayed, the worse the situation became. Everything centered on little Charlie.

Also, Aunt had us to go to her church. We were scared silly, I remember sitting stiffly, hiding my face in my hands, as people became hysterical and screamed and cried. Then, my Dad argued with Aunt, insisting the lady preacher wore a wig. Aunt insisted the lady's hair was all her own, my Dad agreed, saying she no doubt paid for it.

We went to Sunnyside, where we looked at a farm for sale. I, for one, looked at it with dread, there were wooden flumes for carrying water to the fields, but they were half buried under sand.

Fortunately we didn't buy that place. We did buy the forty acres at Ashue, near Wapato. It was situated along one of the big canals and drains, at the time, empty. The house looked good, but turned out to be cold and impossible to heat. There was a garden spot, taken over with raspberries and thistles, now brown and ugly with winter.

Christmas came and for the first time, we had no tree. The wind blew and the sun shone, we went out without coats and had our pictures taken to send to Aunt Sadie and Uncle Dave to show them what a different country we were in.

The boys went to school at Ashue, in a small, white school house. There they met, for the first time, Japanese pupils. Their teachers were a man and wife, who had a grown-up daughter/son who also was a pupil. He-she mainly teased the girls and tattled to his/her parents. He/she was also retarded. The teachers took immediate dislike to my brothers, and they got many whippings, as they were independent and not used to such a situation.

The son/daughter often tattled to his/her mother, she reported to the father and he gave the punishment. The mother even spied on my brothers with field glasses, on their way home. I realize now she probably was jealous, not even realizing herself, because of our normal boys and her own odd offspring.

Our brothers came home reporting some of the kids had lard on their bread, it was un-colored margarine. The first we had ever seen. The depression was being felt by the farmer's first, so we had stepped right into a trap.

Our money for our ranch had gone down, partly by helping Rene's family, and we were cut down in food. The neighbors had their own problems and offered no help, but they did have cows and pigs. One neighbor came with a gallon of skim milk. We had been without milk, so even if it was skimmed, and blue-looking, we appreciated it.

Homesickness set in and with it came every childhood ailment we had missed in Montana. We had chicken pox in Montana, but that was all we'd ever been exposed to. Here in Ashue, we had measles, flu, skin diseases, and some un-recognized illnesses.

It was bad enough to be so far from home without being sick, too. Aunt Rene's kids got chicken pox and as Aunt was in a delicate condition, I was taken to their house to care for the ailing Charlie. It seemed like I rocked him night and day until he got well. Uncle praised me and said he'd pay me a hundred dollars as soon as he got it. He never got it. So, I was put on the list with Virginia, who was waiting for her piano.

Our fields were rocky, and had ditches all over, there was no smooth land. The ditches were a new thing to our folks, so they called it "corrugated land." During the rest of that winter, we hauled rocks away from the fields. We were either sick or picking up rocks. If one could get all the rocks, the farm would be a big hole. It did have a big red barn, where we could play among the rafters like a

An Unusual Childhood

pack of monkeys.

The winter was ugly and grey, part of the time covered with fog. We were used to snow, and bright sunshine in Montana. So, here we were in what Aunt Rene called "God's Country". We were sick, nearly out of money, no friends, and as far as we could see, flat grey land with hay derricks like strange skeletons marching across the unfriendly land.

My Dad chartered a boxcar, and went back to Gardiner, he was gone for some time, but when he got back he had one of our cows, a team of horses; Rock was one of them, and a half-grown filly. Also, he brought the farm machinery we needed, harnesses and other odds and ends. We were so glad to see our cow and the familiar horses. We still had Nicodemus, the dog.

When spring came, we learned about water in the ditches. We planted tomatoes, watermelons and cucumbers; also cantaloupes. When things were up and going good, Daddy discovered he was going to be out of funds. We were given the jobs of hoeing, and Mom became a poor irrigator.

Daddy had a letter asking him to come back to Yellowstone on the Museum building job. As we had to have money, he left for the job. We did quite well for beginners, but the heat was almost more than we could stand; also, the flies. We had never seen so many flies. They formed black masses on the screen door in the evenings.

Finally, we picked the tomatoes and cants, and took them in to sell at Wapato. They told us to take them back and dump them as there was no market. Nothing was sold, as so many people were out of work and not buying anything. In fact, there was no market for any of our produce. Mom got the measles and was so sick she didn't even know us. She talked wildly, so we went to a neighbor and asked to phone a doctor.

He arrived and seemed a little shocked at our way of life, but he left medicine for Mom, and we got money out of Mom's purse and paid him. Mom began to get better, but when she found out we had called a doctor for her, she was really mad.

Harlene Jessie Reeves

She wrote to our Dad and we were jumping with happiness when he wrote back and sent money, to come back to Yellowstone. It seemed all the men had their families with them, and the government had furnished tent houses for the crews and their families. We got Aunt and her family to come and stay at our farm. They were glad to move out of town, Uncle still had no job. There were lines of people in the streets waiting for free loaves of bread.

So we got packed and ready to leave, we took Nicodemus to guard us on the way. This time we were traveling in good weather. We went south to Pasco and headed for Spokane. There were miles and miles of wheat land, and huge whirlwinds, or dust devils; they went every direction and could easily turn a car over if they met. We watched them, but none came near. It was a long, lonely stretch, with only a few houses, and hardly any trees.

When we finally reached Spokane, there were pine trees; they were the most beautiful things we'd seen in a long time. Mom drove all over Spokane, we were lost and using up our gas. We finally found our way out of the suburbs and luckily saw a main road in the distance. We cut across the streets aiming at it, and finally got to the highway.

We entered it in an illegal manner and were on our way, less lots of gas, and wasted time. When darkness came, we got off on a dirt road, ate our lunch and tried to sleep. It was a long night, we tried to settle in the car and sleep, but the boys feet seemed to tangle, or get in someone's face.

We were ready to go when daylight came. We got on a detour that went several dusty miles, trees on both sides and everyone honking car horns because the dust rose so thick and high that it was like driving in thick fog. When we finally came to the highway, as usual, we had lost time.

Mom's theory was to by-pass all big towns, so part of the time we were not sure where we were. We drove until dark, and as usual found a side road, and tried to sleep in the car. After a terrible night of shifting and changing places, and too many feet, gray dawn finally came. To our surprise, we were parked before the gates of the

115

An Unusual Childhood

state Insane Asylum. We left before they opened for business; we probably looked like good prospects for the place.

After getting along quite well for awhile, counting our money, as the price of gas was going up at every stop; we got bread and lunch meat and milk as our daily diet. Mom had just come up over the brow of a hill, and there was a herd of cows in the road, accompanied by a man on horseback.

He managed to get most of them out of the way, as Mom crashed gears and yelled, "Look out!" One old fool cow who thought she owned the road, reared up dead center and straddled our radiator, snorting and angry. We were finally able to stop, the cow got down and joined her herd, but she had broken our headlight. The herder apologized but it didn't fix the light, the cow seemed unhurt, but probably had bruises.

It seemed as though we were never going to get to Yellowstone, although the country was green and there were the trees and it seemed more like home.

It took about three days making this trip, averaging 23-30 miles per hour, of course. It was longer because of Mom's side trips and tours around the cities. When we finally saw the sign for Yellowstone, we were cheered up. This was in Idaho, one of the mining towns. Mom stopped here long enough to look up the Jones family.

They seemed so changed, Helen was boy crazy and Ruby had been sick so didn't seem interested. Earl wasn't around. We didn't try to look up the Webster family because the only one we were interested in, Sylvia's friend, Edna, had died. We didn't like the looks of the country, steep, small hills, honey-combed with mines. The valley was so small that the houses perched on side hills, reached by high stairways. It was not far to the Montana border.

There were still a lot of tiring miles. We finally came to the gates of Yellowstone and felt like leaping out of the car and running ahead, just couldn't wait patiently. Mom was pretty tired after all that driving and plenty glad to dump kids, dog, car and all in Daddy's hands. He had a big army-type tent, with a wooden floor and sides, a big difference from Daddy's old tent used while digging our use-less ditch. We were in the Fishing Bridge Camp, but separated from the tourist's spots. All the workmen and their families were camped nearby.

Our tent was a luxury for just a camp. It had a wood range, beds and screen windows. There was plenty of good firewood near-by, and everyone was allowed a campfire if they wished. There was a grocery store quite close, the prices were so high we could hardly believe it. My Dad often went to Gardiner with his supervisor, so he stocked up with groceries, there.

We sure made up for the hungry days at Ashue; we forgot all about that place. We met the families who were camped near us and the boys made friends with the garbage man and the man who rented boats at the Fishing Bridge. We had the whole beach of Yel-lowstone Lake to pass the time. Most of the time the weather was good—except for the occasional thunderstorms. Even they were something we knew and a great contrast to Ashue.

There were a lot of bears in the park. Most of the time they were just walking about, but a few of them got so tame they became dangerous. At The Lake Hotel, all the garbage was taken to a dump, where, in the evenings the bears appeared and ate like pigs. This was one of the things to see at the Park, in fact there were a lot of wood-en benches for people to sit and watch the bears.

We were there once when a lot of brown and black bears were gobbling their food, when a big grizzly appeared from the trees on the other side of the dump. The other bears must have seen or smelled him, because they all took off and disappeared, except for one little half-grown cub. He was enjoying his meal until he became aware that he was alone. He looked up, saw the big grizzly and darted across the dump, made a fast path through some people and up a tree.

He went up the tree until he had a branch under him, threw a leg over the branch and a front leg around the tree. There he sat, safely high and comfortable and watched the grizzly.

An Unusual Childhood

Another evening, we all went for a power boat ride on the lake. It was a big boat, several families went, I didn't enjoy it, as I had a seat at the back and the cold spray drenched me all the way to and from Stevenson Island.

We met all kinds of people, a Swedish family from Minnesota, a part Indian family from Arizona, an Italian family from Italy, and many people just passing through.

We met and made friends with a girl named Hilda, who had a fat stomach; we formed a clan of the permanent kids, and had lots of things to do. One day we took our lunches and climbed one of the highest hills that looked over Yellowstone Lake. One of the girls was a pest, she brought an umbrella, her rain boots and a coat. We ended up having to carry them and help drag her up the hill; on a nice warm day, too. We didn't include her anymore after that.

Then the people from Italy had this cute, little brat. He was terribly spoiled. One day when our Dad was finishing the beautiful floor in the Museum, the little Italian boy dashed by, and accidentally upset a gallon of paint. My Dad's reaction was a remark, not meant for ladies ears.

The child's mother was chasing her darling down, she caught him and told the little varmint, "You bad, bad boy, you made the nice man say naughty words." He was told to bend over, which he did, and mother slapped his little rear. One thing about the child, he would bend over and take his punishment quite cheerfully.

My brothers caught some nice trout, which they paraded through the tourist campground. They attracted several fish-happy men along the way, who wanted to know how they caught them. They were told that grasshoppers were the best bait, and soon had a thriving business catching and selling grasshoppers.

Mom made friends and they were soon sewing and chattering away. Once, Mom had forgotten her needles and fancy work, which she kept in a child sized chamber pot. She told Clyde to get a needle, the cloth and thread she needed. He got them for her, the whole bit—chamber pot and all. Right through the camps he strolled, getting as much attention as possible.

We had the same system of keeping our groceries, high between two trees, as Daddy did on his ditch camp. One morning, after the dishes were done, Mom put the groceries in the box and pulley-ed it up to its safe-from-bears place. She then discovered she had forgotten her bowl of left-over pan cake batter, so she put it in our Chevrolet; and went to spend part of the day with one of her friends.

When she went back to prepare lunch, there sat a full-sized brown bear in the back seat, he had torn the top off the car and climbed in, where he had eaten and spread batter over the inside of the car as well as himself. Mom turned the dog loose, and opened the car door, then got going away from there. The bear left his seat in a hurry, with the dog barking and practically riding on him. The bear had enough. He went up the first tree that was big enough and stayed. We got the dog back onto the leash, which was the law, and some time later the bear made his escape.

Another time, a bear went right through our tents at night-- in one side and out the other, the boys slept in that section, but were not hurt.

We organized an expedition along the beach to where Pelican Creek entered into the lake. There was a moose feeding in the tall grass, and he evidently didn't want his meal disturbed, at first he just watched us, and then started walking stiff-legged and head high toward us. We Reeves kids had been around cattle enough to realize that meant danger.

We had no escape route, except the lake, which wouldn't stop a water-going moose, but there was a big, gnarled tree nearby. It wasn't long before that tree had a load of scared kids hanging from it. The moose stood guard around the tree, for what seemed like hours, until he forgot what he was mad about and started eating again. He finally wandered off into the trees. We waited a bit longer to be sure he wasn't coming back, then unloaded from the tree and ran for home.

An Unusual Childhood

The boys, in their exploring, found and old rowboat, it was in a thicket of willows and brush near the bridge. Someone had tried to hide it under brush, but it had been there for some time and the brush dried up. The boys brought the boat to our beach, we all got in after it was launched, and using our hands for paddles, we were waterborne, until the boat filled with water and sank.

It was no problem, the boys dived, turned the sunken craft over and it came up. It would be turned right-side-up, everyone get in, and go until it sank again. We never got very far, only to Pelican Creek once. It was tiring, although we enjoyed that boat all summer. No one ever claimed it, so it possibly was stolen. So, it became the property of our gang.

Our Dad worked under Mr. Herb Myers, who took his orders from some of the millionaires back east. Mr. Myers' wife had gone to Europe to have a baby, as many in their class did, so he was often at our tent, he and my Dad grew to be great friends. Once, they were going to Gardiner, when they went around a bend, there was a big, sharp rock in the road.

Mr. Myers had not time to avoid it, and he hit it and blew out a tire. My Dad said he didn't know before that the man knew such colorful languages. They got the tire off, put a patch on, pumped it up, and went on their way. Coming home, rather late from Gardiner, they round the same curve, hit the same rock, and blew another tire. My Dad said that Herb just sat there and laughed.

One day, Mom made a hurried trip to Gardiner, where she got pajamas for the boys, who usually slept whichever way they pleased. The occasion was the visit of two boys, sons of some of the Rockefeller clan. They were visiting Yellowstone and Herb Myers had told their parents or guardians that they would have good care, staying with us. They were quite ordinary boys, but had never seen bacon frying for breakfast. They didn't stay long, as their summer was planned to the last detail.

One day, Daddy had the day off so we got to go back to our old ranch. We were so excited, thinking of all the things we had left behind, and what we would do. It was quite a long trip even for the

Harlene Jessie Reeves

Chev.

When we got to Mammoth, we started pointing out well-re-membered sights. Off in the distance we could see the hills of home. We drove past the Chinese truck gardens, the bridge was gone and the gardens had gone back to native weeds. Another sign of progress.

We went through Gardiner, didn't stop to see Aunt Sadie and Uncle Dave, the day was just not long enough. Even Zee hill out of Gardiner looked good. We went by the Blanding Ranch, now owned by M. Link. It looked as usual. We began to notice that many of the huge granite boulders were cut up and missing.

They had lain scattered, as if a giant had picked them up as pebbles, and scattered them about. The big rock, leaning from the hillside, was still there. The road now was the same as we had left, but grown up with thick grass and weeds. Only Parker's still used it. The gate to our place was open, or missing, and our road was full of weeds.

Our big hay field was badly in need of cutting, but we were all looking forward to seeing our house. Finally, we were there, stopped in the grass-grown yard. Our poor house looked terrible. The windows and doors had been taken away. We darted all through the place, clothing we had left was all over the place, the books from our bookcase, were strewn about the floor and out the open front door, they were ruined by the rain and weather.

We went in the garage, or what was left of it, and hunted for our skis, but they were gone, as was part of the garage. Sylvia dis-covered two black overcoats, still hanging in the downstairs closet. We took them. Our folks evidently felt very unhappy with the way our old home looked, and we left, but were indignant about the way things had changed. Mostly, we were very quiet on the way back to camp. Getting back late, we had not much to say, we would have been better off not to have gone back.

Sylvia had the black overcoats; they were heavy wool, so she made us each a jacket. I didn't sew mine as nicely as Sylv's, I remem-ber, I even used white thread, and they were all done with needle

121

and thread. The weather was getting cooler and the jackets felt pretty good.

One day Clyde told us that people were referring to us as the "Black Jackets." Sylvia didn't like that too well.

The weather was getting colder, soon the Park would be closed, and the opening of school was nearing. That meant we had to go back to Ashue. The trip wasn't very eventful; Mom still had a bad time finding her way through the cities along the way.

As we were entering Missoula, Mom drove to the side of the road, and greatly amused passing travelers by getting the hot-cake turner, and giving the boys each a good whipping. They were trapped in the back seat, and their fighting and bright remarks were too much. Mom had enough trouble driving through a strange city without comments from behind.

We were home in time for school, and I got a prune-picking job to buy my books and school clothes. The Depression was pinching everyone; we had to buy our school books. Sylvia had started school, so I was about 2 weeks behind her. When I went in to enroll into the ninth grade, I wanted to go by myself. Mom talked to the Principal. I was assigned a home room.

I told Mom I could find it, but she wanted to help me, the school seemed so huge, with long, gleaming halls, and room after room full of students. Mom got me by the hand and practically dragged me along. I tried resisting, she probably thought I would break and run, so we entered together.

The class was already studying, the room was quiet when Mom and I entered everyone became alert. Mom towed me up to the teacher's desk. "This is my girl," she told him, giving him the necessary papers. I was red-faced. I had become fat on our starchy diet, also had my hair cut in a "boyish bob," a popular style, but on me it was a mess. Also, dear Aunt Rene had made a dress for me, it had a gathered skirt, and 3 tiers of ruffles gathered on the skirt. It was the worst thing I could have worn.

Harlene Jessie Reeves

I was assigned a seat and Mom left, I wanted to leave, too. That first day was one of the worst I have ever spent, I was lost, couldn't' find my rooms when the classes changed. I met with the lockers, with combination locks, and it didn't help when a girl with a wart on her eyelid, and buck teeth, came up to me and asked if I was a Dago.

Everything happened to me, I got on the right bus to go home, the bus was divided down the center, boys on one side, girls on the other. The bus was driven by a volunteer student who had no control over his passengers. The boys were always fighting.

One afternoon, on the way home, the boys were throwing a bottle of ink around, it came sailing towards me, and I threw up my hand to ward it off--it rebounded, the cork came out, and the ink splattered the whole front of one of the high school girls. She happened to be wearing a new dress. She was very sweet about it, and didn't blame me.

All these days seemed to be my memories of Ashue, hard work, not enough to eat, very few new clothes. Then the summer, blazing hot, hoeing tomatoes, or watermelons; and our filly died of a strange skin disease, and probably homesickness.

Sylvia had a heat stroke in the tomato field, Mom was sick half of the time; she hated the heat and the flat, rocky farm. We were plenty glad when Daddy was called back to Yellowstone. He made a better living there than he could do on the farm. When we got there we met most of the same people, it was like a home-coming.

We didn't go back to the ranch, again. Someone told us that the house was gone, but I didn't believe it. One day, I had gone to the store for something, and there were a lot of people with horses and pack horses. They were getting supplies for a trip into the back country of the park.

The riders rode out, single file, and then I saw Dot! She looked well taken care of and a lady was riding her. I know it was Dot, there were not likely to be many horses with the scarred front foot. It made me both happy and sad. She looked so well, and was no

An Unusual Childhood

longer my horse.

I decided that when I grew up, I would move back to Gardiner, at least. But fate didn't work out that way; it was thirty years later when I finally did go back. Burly went back often, as he lived in Missoula. Bud went back for a time and met his future wife, LaVee, there.

Sylvia got back there and her son Dennis and his family accompanied her. Dennis insisted on making a grave marker for Perry's grave. He also struck up a conversation with any of the old people he met. My parents went back, after my Dad retired.

They were terribly disappointed; my Dad said all he could find was a rim off an old wheel; he put it with a rusted wrench, where he said they could be together. Clyde and family went once--Clyde said everything seemed so small, the roads were changed and everything had been changed, even Eagle Creek was no more--it had been renamed Davis Creek. The elevation bothered some of the family members.

Finally, the summer of 1968, our younger son, Paul, and a friend named Judd Williams were left in charge of our family farm and my husband, Bill, my daughter Gail and I were off to Montana. Burly had enticed Bill into the hobby of hunting old bottles, and we went with them to the mountain-top-high city of Granite, Montana, an old silver mining ghost town.

The country is in the Rocky Mountains, and beautiful. Some of the best farm country in Montana is far behind in farming methods and machinery, but they don't care. The fishing is nearby, and also hunting. We saw a lot of older methods of stacking hay, some beautiful cattle and fresh, cool air. After we left Livingston, Montana, I was surprised the highway was on the opposite side of the river.

We stopped at the Old Tavern, an old, white building, still serving drinks, where the owner-operator has two of my Grandmother Jennie Davis' paintings. He knew Mom and my Aunts as teenagers.

124

Harlene Jessie Reeves

I hated to tell him that Aunt Winnie had died and Mom was in a nursing home. We went on to Gardiner, where we saw Elk in a corral. We crossed the new bridge; Aunt Sadie's house was gone. Zee hill was the same, but was nothing to a modern pick-up truck.

We went by the Blandings, now known as Blandings Station. Then came the big changes: Our old road was gone! There was a good timbering road across our former horse pasture; it crossed Davis Creek, passed the old Austrian's Gulch and went way up into the mountains. There were no landmarks of any kind to show civilization.

We camped above where our house had been, the whole yard area was a mess of nettles and weeds, the spring had spread and no longer ran in a polite little stream into Eagle (Davis) Creek. All that was left of the house was a square outline of rocks where our cellar had been. Our side-hill root cellar was only a sunken place in the hill, grown up with weeds. There was no trace of a barn, sheds, or anything; even the fences, posts, wires and all were as though they had never been.

The bridge was gone and so was the lane to our house. I found a part of a buggy wheel, it came home with us. We did find our old heating stove, sitting under a tree. We poked around. I found a small weather-shrunken boy's shoe, one of my brother's. Gail ran off up the creek and dug up some old things; we were looking at them, and sitting on a fallen tree, when I discovered the sleigh we used to travel in. It was crushed underneath the tree that had fallen.

We left there and drove up to Casey's Lake; it was the same, as was the pond where the ducks were always scared up when we were riding to school. We found the remains of Casey's house and Bill found some of Casey's machinery, still in working condition.

The girls looked down the mountain where we used to ride, and we could see the old, white schoolhouse. Everywhere the grass was thick and untouched. The elk that had to have that range had been so depleted because the new government policy was to butcher the herds and send the meat back east. The country was wasted as far as game was concerned. Many people were uprooted for no reason. We didn't have enough time; we did want to get to Parkers as they were gone, too.

The grass was matted and high with year after year and no elk, cattle or horses to feed on it. There are a few horses; they stood in the shade of the big trees where Mrs. Parker and her baby lie. We went up to where the horse corral was, there wasn't a trace of it, only the water trough, which had washed partly down the hill, and the corral itself was grown up with trees.

My Dad's initials were carved upon a tree, and Sylvia's, grown so high she couldn't have reached them, now. I put my "Harl" on one of these trees.

This whole area was swampy and full of mosquitoes that were starving. I don't know where all that water came from; perhaps it had been drained off before everything had been abandoned. The view, though, was as good as ever. We could see the white geyser formations, steam and all, in the far distance.

The next day we returned to the Park entrance at Gardiner. I recognized the Scotts' house, the garage where we looked at new cars and many other things. Of course, my family didn't recognize anything.

We joined the thousands of tourists traveling from all over the nation looking for recreation, bears, fish, deer, elk, moose, and so on. We did see a few elk in the distance, and one near a river. There were several mooching bears and a man caught a fish from Yellow-stone Lake.

We went to the Fishing Bridge; the old bridge was gone, with its rows of fishermen on both sides. The new un-friendly bridge bore a sign saying, "NO FISHING". We found the museum, one of those my Dad had helped to build. The little evergreens that had been set out to beautify the building were huge trees, they had cracked the concrete, but the building was the same.

In one of the glass cases, was our old friend, the hawk. He sat forever, glaring and perching on a dead bough. I knew him instantly and wondered where the Kingfisher sat.

We saw new geysers where there had been none before, and some of the remembered ones no longer were in action. There were people everywhere, where once was solitude, and wild animals. Where we used to run along boards between one attraction to another, there now was a sturdy boardwalk and warning signs for all the milling people.

We were at Old Faithful Camp, where we were to phone home to see if things were okay. People were waiting for the geyser to erupt on time, since it had done since the place was first discovered.

Bill was phoning Paul, where he said the temperature was 109 degrees, and where we were in a sudden storm; thunder, lightning, rain—the works. People were running for shelter. It was one of the nicest storms I had seen for a long time; but it stopped and the air was fresh and cool.

All too soon, for me, we had to start for home. We were somewhere near Virginia City when we saw the sign, Spokane, so many miles. Bill remarked we were an awful long way from home.

This time, though, I had looked back. The house and outer buildings were gone, the fences, the paths and road, it was as though it had never been. But the town, Gardiner, and the old mining town, Jardine are still there, the people are changed; they don't mine for gold, but most of them work for the government in Yellowstone, where progress is ruining one of the most unusual Parks in the Nation.

Also, the hills, Crevasses, Teddy's Hill, Porcupine Jim, and Grey Donkey are still there and will probably always be there. Eagle Creek is there, whether it's known as Davis Creek or not, it will always be singing its way down through the valley. Buffalo Flats will not be known by that name, as it is re-named; and the old cemetery, with "Welcome" at the gates.

127

An Unusual Childhood

Our Dad's ditch will probably eventually fill in; it is merely a scar across Teddy's Hill, now. But, Mike L., the same man who bought the Blanding ranch, is the only one who gained anything from the ditch. Perry's grave and the graves of Mrs. Parker and her baby will always be there, and perhaps there will always be a few wild horses to doze under the big trees.

Burl and some of his family go back quite often, they mended the picket fence under the big trees, but no doubt, some horse will push it down.

Gail loved the country; she threatened to write to Washington DC about their muddling projects. She considered trying to buy the place back, when she was older and if it was allowed. She probably has dropped the idea, but when the summer gets hot in the Yakima Valley, I often envy Burl, who goes back every summer. He looks up Mary M. and others. I wouldn't even know them.

Sylvia knows many more and recognizes the places we used to live, even the Cedar Creek place where Clyde was born and where we were shut in a cellar, as a punishment. She remembers people's names and where they are now. Her son, Dennis, was very interested, and even urged Sylvia to talk to the older people, and get their stories. Many of them were old friends of our parents and knew where some of them were.

Uncle Dave lies buried at the Gardiner Cemetery, Aunt Sadie in a family plot somewhere back east. My Dad told me that Horace Labree looked as if he had already died and forgotten to fall down. I don't know what happened to our friends Ruth Ellen and Amy. We heard that Geraldine had married a widower with a lot of children; let's hope she treated them better than her horses.

Mr. Parker had become an alcoholic, and the last time we heard anything about him was he had been in a drunken rage and ran the twin, Jiggs, out in the middle of winter and that she had run bare-footed all the way to the Blandings. Mrs. Morrison, of the Fur Farm, is gone and Louise's parents were living in the big house.

Harlene Jessie Reeves

Our old house in Jardine is the office of a wrecking yard; it is surrounded by junked cars. One of the mills had burned down. I've not wanted to go back to Jardine, there is too much changed. I know Mom was depressed when she went back, even though her younger sister had moved back.

I would like to go back, when we have more time: Time to go up where we had our old trails, to the old mill -or where it was - and follow the ditch line. I would like Paul to go, he might enjoy it. Perhaps we could pick up some obsidian arrow heads that we found so often and carelessly threw away. It would be nice to drink some of the cold, clean water from the spring or the creek, and look across the miles to Mammoth Hot Springs in Yellowstone Park.

But the people we knew and neighbors we had are gone. I once read a book from the Junior High library, concerning the wildlife in Montana. Part of it was about the Elk and their gradually thinning herds. The author mentioned bear hunting, and visiting with a guide to the back country, "He was one of the finest men I have ever known, his name was Dave Rhodes." I was pleased to meet our old friend, even in a book.

I believe I had an unusual childhood and in this rushed and harried day of civilization, I wish my own daughters and sons could have had a part of our life, on Eagle Creek, in Montana.

The end

Epilogue

My mother, Harlene Jessie Reeves Ritchie, wrote this, years ago, in a blank book that Gail, one of my sisters, gave to her. This is the only e-book version, produced after Mom died in 2001.

I am her first son. My name is Bill, like my Dad's. Lynda (my wife) and I had Mom's original hand-written book for a few months, and we enjoyed reading it. We had a practice of reading books aloud to each other, just before turning in. This was relaxing—far better than TV and as good reading as published novels. Mom's hand-written book was one of the best we read. It had only one drawback, and that was that sometimes her stories made us laugh so hard it was difficult to settle down and go to sleep.

From reading her stories, I thought of a background note: It was a common belief (according to Mom in her childhood days) that babies came from Sears Roebuck, as did calves, colts and all other newborns. We know better, now. We know that babies do not come from Sears & Roebuck (because Sears stopped publishing its mail order catalog). Newborns come from a big love factory somewhere in heaven.

I think all joys of life come from a big factory that makes such love as that kind we inherit from our parents and grandparents. In this spirit, I take the words from my Mother's story and, with the help of my sister, Gail (who put the handwritten text in a computer-readable form) I am making it more accessible.

Our Mom's story might be read aloud to spouses and special other persons and enjoyed and shared. She tells her story so well about how things used to be in her childhood days in Montana and later when she lived in the Yakima Valley in Washington.

Epilogue

Harlene Jessie Reeves (Ritchie)
Photo taken about 1935, Wapato, Washington

Born 1916 - Passed 2001

Cow Pasture W. of House

Cows

Yellowstone Park building Harlene's Dad, Harley, worked on.

Epilogue

Taken from Grey Donkey Mtn — looking
at Teddy's Hill

Ridge E. of House

Cow Pasture — Gray Donkey Hill in
Distance

selves. We were all invited to a party. I didn't want to go as my shoes were boy's shoes and plenty worn, we scoured thru our clothes and I found a pair of girl's sleppers, none of us knew how they got there, we had never seen them before, but they just fit me, so I went to the party after all. There was a big cake and ice cream, and each of us won a gift, by winning a game. I won a pair of pepper and salt shakers, very small and pretty. I still have them.

Finally spring came, we

Harlene's story on winning the salt and pepper set, pictured here.

Epilogue

When I am facing a major illness, broken bones or surgery, I say to myself "this too shall pass", and it usually does.

My dad was born in Wycliffe, Kentucky. His parents were Nancy Wings and Sydney Reeves. He had a half-brother, Burley Douhett, and three sisters, Lynn, Lurley and lady Margaret, brothers, Clyde, Hubbard, Brian.

He had five children, Sylvia, Harlene, Burley, Clyde and Bud.

My mother was born in Montana. Her parents were Winifred and Jennie Cutler Davis. She had two brothers Charles and Earl, and four sisters, Winifred, Naomi, Irene and Ivy (Babe).

My dad and Burley co-owned a saloon in Gardiner Montana, they put up with gun fights. In fact one of Jennie Davis paintings has a bullet hole in it. It was hanging in the saloon. It is presently owned by one of my brother Burleys daughters.

Our family moved to granpa Davis hunting lodge. Granma and grandpa moved to Yellowstone park, where aunt Babe and husband lived. We did live on Buffalo Flat, It was remote and infested with rattle snake. Sylvia and were born there.

Harlene's handwrtten notes from her journal.

135

www.ingramcontent.com/pod-product-compliance
Lightning Source LLC
Chambersburg PA
CBHW060940040426
42445CB00011B/944

9 781562 359058